DRY STONE WALLING

materials and techniques

T0272425

DRY STONE WALLING

materials and techniques

NICK AITKEN

THE CROWOOD PRESS

First published in 2023 by
The Crowood Press Ltd
Ramsbury, Marlborough
Wiltshire SN8 2HR

enquiries@crowood.com

www.crowood.com

© Nick Aitken 2023

All rights reserved. No part of this publication may be reproduced or transmitted in any form or by any means, electronic or mechanical, including photocopy, recording, or any information storage and retrieval system, without permission in writing from the publishers.

British Library Cataloguing-in-Publication Data
A catalogue record for this book is available from the British Library.

ISBN 978 0 7198 4167 5

Photos contributed by: Lluc Mir Anguera; Daniel Arabella; Dry Stone Conservancy, Jane M. Wooley; Drystone Walling Perthshire, Martin Tyler; John Bland; Sean Donnelly; Jared Flynn; Neil Rippingale; Ben Schultz; Maya Stessin; Nicolette Stessin; David F. Wilson.

Typeset by Simon and Sons
Cover design by Blue Sunflower Creative
Printed and bound in India by Parksons Graphics

Contents

Dedication and Preface   6

Chapter One   The Development of Dry Stone Walling   7

Chapter Two   Types of Rock, Sources and Quantities   13

Chapter Three   The Basics of Working with Stone   23

Chapter Four   Laying, Trimming and Securing Stone   38

Chapter Five   Constructing a Dry Stone Wall   50

Chapter Six   A Gallery of Wall Types and Bonding Patterns   88

Chapter Seven   Special Circumstances and Obstacles   108

Chapter Eight   Repairing a Gap   142

Chapter Nine   Retaining Walls   152

Chapter Ten   Openings, Arches and Roofs   159

Chapter Eleven   Modern Walling: Pushing the Boundaries   172

Chapter Twelve   Practical Advice for the Novice   180

Chapter Thirteen   A Final Challenge   183

Glossary   185

Bibliography   187

Useful Addresses   189

Index   190

A Dedication

I dedicate this book to my wife Nicolette, and the wallers and dykers who generously shared images and information about their work. The craft is in safe hands.

A Preface

Georg Müller (2013) estimated there were 520,552 miles (837,750km) of dry stone walls in the British Isles in 1880, which would have taken 1.9 billion man hours to build. Many of these walls no longer exist. Most were built by teams of contractors in the eighteenth and nineteenth centuries. There were no formal apprenticeships. Wallers learned on the job, guided by experienced men whose skills were obvious, yet difficult to define.

In 2018, UNESCO recognized the walling skills of Croatia, Cyprus, France, Greece, Italy, Slovenia, Spain and Switzerland by adding dry stone walling to the representative list of the Intangible Cultural Heritage of Humanity. This acknowledges the expertise of wallers and their contribution to the cultural landscape, wherever they work.

We constantly hear that dry stone walling is 'a dying art' (a refrain since the 1930s). Nowadays, with the benefits of international communication, a huge database and an increase in the awareness of environmental and conservation issues, there is ample evidence that the craft is alive and safe, in the hands of several international dry stone walling associations.

Whether you are a complete novice, or a waller with some experience, this book aims to provide you with some, or more, insight into the historic development and building methodology of dry stone walling, and inspire you with examples of new structures built using only stone, held together with friction, gravity, symmetry and balance.

Whatever your level of experience, the ideal way to develop the skill is to do it. Contact your local walling association (details at the back of the book) and take part in their training events or monthly gatherings. Join a stone festival, like Northstone Stonefest in Caithness, Scotland, or those in western Ireland and throughout North America and Europe. These cultural experiences offer the opportunity to learn, establish contacts and become a part of the larger stone community.

Dry stone walling has a specific and specialized terminology. Hopefully the terms are self-explanatory within the text, but some can be clarified using the cross-section on page 51 and the glossary towards the end of this book.

Chapter One

The Development of Dry Stone Walling

Dry stone walls are termed 'dry stone dykes', 'drystane dykes' or simply 'dykes' in Scotland. The terms are used interchangeably in the following text, depending on the location of the structure.

A Brief History

Dry stone walls are a common feature in the British landscape, dividing fields and crossing moorlands, creating an impressive network of human endeavour. What we see today is a relatively recent addition, most of it built since 1700. The earliest agricultural walls were not sophisticated but they were effective, although they were often little more than rows of large stones, set on edge, with smaller stones between.

Dry stone construction is an ancient building technique that does not use any type of mortar. It relies on friction and gravity to keep stone in its set position.

Ancient Walls

Indigenous cultures have built with stone for thousands of years. They built dry stone fish traps, irrigation systems, livestock enclosures and hunting hides all over the world, including the Middle East, southern Africa, Australia and North America. The likelihood of these cultures interconnecting is remote, therefore this type of construction is an excellent example of an instinctive use of local material by a wide range of local peoples.

There is a long history of building with stone in the British Isles. The buried walls in the Céide Fields in County Mayo, Ireland are the remains of a Neolithic farming system dating back about 5,000 years (McAfee, 2011). No description of mortarless stone construction can go without mentioning Maes Howe and Scara Brae in the Orkney islands. These structures, at 5,000 years, are as old as the Egyptian pyramids at Giza.

The earliest walls at Roystone Grange, in Derbyshire, England likely date back more than 3,000 years (Hodges, 1991). The landscape around the Grange includes evidence of ancient stone walls and much younger walls; stones were recycled over the ages as farming practices changed.

Gallarus Oratory and Skellig Michael in Ireland date back nearly 2,000 years.

In Malham, North Yorkshire, stone walls date back to the thirteenth and fourteenth centuries (Lord, 2004). They were built round the monastic sheep pastures to protect their sheep and their wool profits. These walls had less batter, were nearly vertical, and not so refined as the dry stone wall types that were built since the 1600s.

Apart from the walls round these monastic sheep farms and hunting grounds, most walls prior to the seventeenth century were described as ephemeral or seasonal. They protected the summer crops, required a lot of maintenance and were often allowed to collapse in the winter. Livestock, mainly cattle at that time, were kept on the common grazing land and only allowed into the cultivated areas during the winter, to clear up what was left in the fields after harvest.

An older style of dry stone wall, with upright slabs and small stones, in ruinous state. This structure uses available stone in the most efficient way. Age unknown. North Uist, Scottish Hebrides.

A Need for Permanent Boundaries

A radical reorganization of agricultural in Great Britain started in the seventeenth century. The Enclosure Acts stripped smallholders of their rights to graze on the common pastures and, in the name of efficiency, passed the ownership to fewer and fewer landlords, who set themselves up to make a good income from wool, beef and grain. Setting boundaries became important, and there was a need for reliable field boundaries to protect crops and livestock. A more permanent walling system was required.

Various systems of ditches and mounds of earth, sometimes faced with stone and a hedge, were tried. Hedges were one answer but they were slow growing. One development was the turf and stone dyke. This wall was easily constructed out of the local rock, and the turf cut from the foundation trench. There was no need to calculate a tight fit, as the weight of the stones squeezed the turf into the gaps. This type of wall was robust and required less maintenance than previous walls or fences, but it had one obvious disadvantage – it used turf stripped from

the pasture, in addition to the turf cut for the foundation. This was valuable grazing that took a year or more to fully regrow. On some rocky ground, it might not even have been possible to find enough turf for such a wall.

Rainsford-Hannay (1976) tells us dry stone dyking, the building of freestanding dry stone walls as we know it today, was first developed in southwest Scotland around 1700.

Dry stone walls were an important development in agricultural fencing. They were a universal answer to a universal need, made from a cheap local material. A stone wall has many advantages over a hedge or a wooden fence: it provides good shelter, is durable, and easily built out of local materials by local workers. Possible downsides are that it is immovable, can harbour pests and takes up too much room.

Thousands of miles of fencing were required as agriculture reorganized into large estates with tenant farmers. Boundaries had to be defined over remote moors and hillsides. Mortared walls were a possibility, but the costs and inconveniences of lime mortar (the only option at that time) made them expensive.

A turf and stone dyke or 'feal dyke', named for an old Scots word for turf. This easily constructed combination of materials is an ideal starter home for rabbits. Highland Folk Museum, Newtonmore, Scotland.

Older styles of mortarless stone walls existed; they were finessed to produce a permanent structure that could be relied on to protect boundary lines and livestock bloodlines.

Early commentators wrote passionately about the benefits of dry stone walls, emphasizing the importance of batter, copes, throughstones and hearting. These elements were already well known to the builders of ancient stone structures, and the masons who built mortared walls. They were now applied to the construction of slim, tall agricultural walls.

This new type of dry stone wall was what we now call the standard free-standing 'double wall' (*see* box). Agricultural commentators in the eighteenth and nineteenth centuries advocated this design both at home and in agricultural journals overseas.

It was a teachable process and a growing workforce specialized in building them. Many regional variations evolved, depending on the local geology. The basic design was flexible, and adaptable enough to suit every region, from the limestones and siltstones of northern Scotland to the granites of the Cairngorms and the limestones of the English Cotswolds. Walling became a skilled trade, rather than a part-time job.

Wall Building at its Peak

Meanwhile, the farmers in Europe and North America were developing their own styles of wall. Europeans especially developed retaining walls. The amount

Two Main Types of Wall

A single dyke, one stone thick, built using boulders. It was constructed from left to right, up the slight slope. This would also be described as a 'boulder dyke'. Some of the top stones have fallen, but this is an easy repair. Southwest Scotland.

A section across a double dyke, clearly showing its most important feature – the two outer skins of face stones and the smaller stones (hearting) in the middle. Protruding throughstones are visible in the background. The copestones have been dislodged. Knoydart, Scotland.

A **double wall** or dyke consists of two outer faces of carefully laid stone, usually with long narrow stones (throughstones) connecting the faces at approximately half height. An arrangement of coverband and copestones caps the wall off. The interior of the wall is filled with hearting – smaller angular stones that secure the larger face stones. This type of wall is typically 28in (71cm) wide at grass level and 14in (36cm) wide under the copestones. The cope is usually formed out of flatter stones set vertically on edge. The total height might be 4–5ft (1.2–1.5m) for walls round arable fields, and taller for boundary walls between estates. These are by far the most common type of wall.

The **single wall** or dyke is the best way to use up large stones or boulders. This style of construction is one stone wide, from bottom to top. The largest stones are laid as a foundation course. Smaller stones are laid on top of that, until the wall reaches the required height, which can be 4–5ft (1.2–1.5m), and not much wider than a double wall. If a single wall is built with mechanical assistance, it can be up to 11ft (3.5m) high (MacWeeney and Conniff, 1998).

There are also 'triple' walls. This term is used to describe double walls with another face of stone laid up against them, to use up stone cleared from the fields.

of dry stone field walling in Europe should not be underestimated. Georg Müller's calculations (2013) for the year 1880 show that France, Greece and Spain each had more dry stone field walls than Great Britain and Northern Ireland. Sweden, a country we do not usually associate with such walls, had only slightly less.

The 1800s were a busy time for wallers. Fortunes were made in the wool trade, on both sides of the Atlantic. Stone walls were essential for management of sheep.

Kentucky benefited from the – mainly Irish – immigrants who built miles of free-standing double-faced dry stone walls out of the local limestone. Scottish and Irish wallers worked for Australian sheep stations.

The New Englanders tidied up the accumulated stones round the edges of their fields to build their own unique style – low, wide walls with flat slabs across the top. There is no question that during the construction of these walls they were recycling some stone used by earlier indigenous people for their walls.

By the early 1900s, however, dry stone walling was in decline, as most of the walls that were needed had been built; consequently, wallers tended to concentrating on maintenance work. Newspaper articles from before 1939 were lamenting the decline of the craft and the loss of another country skill. This trend has now reversed. Awareness of dry stone walling is increasing around the world, and many old walls are being restored by conservation groups. Patrons are willing to support high-end projects – work that still uses the traditional methods of construction but with more detailing and greater accuracy.

The Influence of Local Geology

There are as many types of wall as there are types of stone. Walls look different because each stone type has characteristics that dictate how it can be used. No matter how the wall is built or the stone type used, they all rely on the same basic principle: a stone, properly laid, in solid contact with its neighbours, will not move.

The type of wall, and how it is built, depends on the available stone. For three centuries, local wallers have used their local stone the most efficient way they could to produce a stock-proof fence. No time was wasted on unnecessary detail.

Dry stone walls in the mountains of Scotland or northern England use rougher stone, and look rougher, because that's the local geology. They look

very different, but serve nearly the same function as the more precise limestone walls in the south of England.

Another factor influencing the style of wall is, of course, the job they do. The mountain walls were built to enclose agile sheep and declare boundary lines. They are consequently more substantial than the walls around arable fields in the valleys.

There are areas in Great Britain where stone is in short supply, for example southeast England. By happy accident these are usually the milder areas of the country where hedges grow easily, and these are an ideal option for agricultural fencing.

Some rock types naturally occur as easily handled pieces with regular sizes, shapes and angles. Other types require breaking or shaping before they can be used. A large stone can be manageable if it is square and flat, while a smaller stone will be awkward if it is angular with no obvious centre of gravity. Small, flat stones are easily handled and built into refined walls, but big boulders or flat slabs require more work and imagination.

Big pieces of rock, whether they are boulders or slabs of limestone, are most often used 'as found' – for example in single walls or as in the limestone feidín walls of western Ireland (see Chapter 6). If there is good mix of large and small stones, the larger stones are often spread out at regular intervals or set as upright slabs – 'bookends' for the smaller stones.

Wallers took advantage of any really large stones lying along the route of the wall. Early dry stone walling was a matter of building as much as possible, as quickly as possible. Wallers in the eighteenth and nineteenth centuries were usually paid by the yard. It was easy money for them if a huge boulder could be levered into position to make an instant yard or two. One relatively easy way to move a large boulder sitting on solid ground is to throw some smaller stones under it and push away with crowbars. The small stones reduce the contact between the boulder and the ground, and less contact means less friction and less energy required to move it.

High and Handsome

This 5ft (1.5m) enclosure wall most likely dates back to the early 1800s. It was built with stone pulled from the ground, gathered from the hillside or recycled from older structures. Large pieces were set on end and some were laid traced — that is, with their long edge along the wall. This does not create a weakness in this instance, as the size of the stones renders normal placement rules obsolete. The two 'pillars' in this vertical wall are unlikely to be gateposts — just two stones put into positions where they could best assist their smaller comrades. The face we see was built vertical; the other side of the wall is built with a batter and it narrows towards the top.

The lichen growth on the copestones confirms this is an old, undisturbed, wall. St Kilda, Scotland.

Chapter Two

Types of Rock, Sources and Quantities

Rock Types

To some extent the words 'rock' and 'stone' are interchangeable. Rock is a general term for part of the earth's crust; a stone is part of that crust, broken down or shaped so that it can be used for building.

Most rock types have a high compressive strength, meaning they are difficult to crush when piled on top of each other. This makes them an ideal building material.

It is useful to understand a rock type, its origins and limitations, before working out how to break or shape it.

In general terms, there are three rock types, named for their method of origin.

Some rocks are formed from magma (molten rock under the earth's crust) or lava (magma expelled by volcanic activity). Others are formed by the slow accumulation of sediments from the erosion of those rocks. The first of these are called igneous rocks, the second are sedimentary rocks. Both types were often subjected to extreme pressure or heat to form new rocks or broken, shattered varieties of the original. These are called metamorphic rocks.

Igneous Rocks

Igneous rocks are the oldest rocks, created from cooled lava or magma. Magma is molten rock under the earth's crust. Lava is the same material pushed to the surface, commonly seen as a red-hot mass pouring down the side of a volcano. Magma cools more slowly under the earth's crust, so there is plenty of time for crystals to form as it does so, producing rough-grained rocks such as gabbro or granites.

When magma is pushed above the earth's crust, as lava, it produces finer-grained rocks such as basalt and andesite. It cools relatively quickly, so there is less time for crystals to form.

Volcanic activity also produces various forms of ash. Some types consolidate to form a soft rock called tuff, which is easily shaped and therefore a good building material.

Basalt columns, a common form of this igneous rock. It is dense, hard, brittle, and easily broken down into smaller pieces. Oregon, USA.

Igneous rocks formed many of the mountainous areas in Scotland, northern England and Wales, and were duly incorporated into the sturdy mountain walls we see today.

Sedimentary Rocks

Sedimentary rocks are the result of the build-up of sediments over millions of years. Silts, muds and biological debris accumulated on ocean bottom and lake beds, and were bound together by natural cements. In their purest form, sedimentary rocks appear with distinctly coloured layers, separated by bedding planes, where one thin line represents thousands of years of geological activity. The bedding plane can be a line of weakness: the rock is easier to split along these planes. These rocks are associated with gentler geological eras, when material had time to settle without disturbance.

Sedimentary rock types include limestone, coal, sandstone, siltstones, shale and conglomerates. Conglomerate rocks are types of sandstone with a substantial percentage of larger rounded or angular material within the silts; they sometimes look like a broken piece of concrete.

Most sandstones have a parallel top and bottom edge. They are easily cut and shaped to make tightly coursed walls. The quarries in Caithness, northern Scotland, process a type of fine sandstone, a siltstone,

A limestone wall in western Ireland. This sedimentary rock is pried off the ground, or from outcrops, in relatively flat pieces. The walling style is derived from the rock – often large slabs laid on edge, with a rough cope, or built one stone thick, with the minimum of cutting or shaping. The Burren, Ireland.

Could this sandstone cliff face be described as 'solid rock'? The sedimentary beds are weather-beaten and eroded. Plants take advantage of splits and ledges. This could be an easily worked source of stone. Berriedale, Scotland.

which breaks out into big flagstones. Acres of quarry floor produce predictable thicknesses of stone, which are ideal for paving and, laid upright on edge, also make a good flagstone fence.

Sedimentary rocks do not always consist of small-grained material. Beds of rougher rock sometimes lie between layers of finer grained rock. It depends on how the grains got there. Wind may have blown sands and dusts to form one layer, while water carried larger-grained material to sit on top of that. The upper stretches of ancient river beds have coarser material in their sediments because pebbles and large-grained sands fell to the bottom first. The smaller, lighter material was washed downstream to lakes and seas, to where it settled and was eventually compressed into fine-grained sandstones. The face of a sandstone quarry can resemble a marble cake.

Some sedimentary rocks, particularly sandstones and limestones, contain fossils. These are not found in igneous rock (because of its fiery origin), or were destroyed by the heat or pressures that created metamorphic rocks.

Metamorphic Rocks

Geology is an ongoing process. Metamorphic rock types were created after tremendous heat and pressure altered igneous and sedimentary rocks. They often have bands of colouring or crystals, brought about by the pressures that formed them. Types include schist, quartzite, gneiss, slate and marble. They are often granular and break into rough sheets.

Boulders

Any rock type, apart from possibly the softer rocks, can appear as boulders. In geological terms, a boulder is a piece of stone more than 10in (25cm) in diameter. In walling terms, we think of them as the large rounded stones found in river beds, floodplains and sand quarries.

Boulders began as pieces of bedrock torn from the larger mass. Their edges were then rounded by glacial and water action. Boulders retain the original characteristics of the rock they broke away from, so, for example, granite boulders are heavy and not easily split, while sandstone boulders will break along sedimentary planes.

Urbanite

This is a modern term applied to broken concrete, usually in the form of slabs. If it is a decent size with

A single or single-skinned dry stone dyke built from whole and split boulders. The spectacularly level top line shows what can be built from rough material, probably using nothing more complex than hammers and a length of string. Southwest Scotland.

An urbanite retaining wall on a corner. In the background we see one of the city's many retaining walls, constructed from blocks of basalt. Seattle, USA.

good faces, it can be used, like any flat stone, to make free-standing walls, retaining walls or paving. It can be very similar in appearance to conglomerate sandstone – a type of sandstone consisting of silts and large aggregate, all bonded together with natural cements such as calcite or quartz. The broken face of these slabs looks unattractive but they trim easily and weather quickly. Lime leaching from the concrete will also be beneficial to local plant growth.

If broken concrete is irregular and reasonably sized, it could be used for backing up retaining walls, especially if the stone for the face of the wall is expensive. Retaining walls should be wide and heavy; there is no need to spend money on expensive rock if it is placed at the back, invisible forever.

Sourcing Stone

The early wallers and dykers working on agricultural dry stone walls had a ready supply of stone along the route of the wall they were building. Stone cleared from the land was reformed into walls. If necessary, additional stone was brought in from nearby quarries or rock outcrops, or prised from stream beds. Using the local rock was always the best option, as carrying stone any distance was expensive and added considerably to the cost of a new wall.

Old buildings or old walls are a good source of building material. Stone from many old structures, including Hadrian's Wall, found their way into dry stone walls during the eighteenth century, when a

This south-facing slope illustrates how much effort went into clearing land. The crofters (smallholder farmers) removed the stones to the edge of their ground, forming ridges and roughly built walls. The land between is remarkably clear of stone. Ullapool, Scotland.

boom in wall construction followed the reorganization of land holdings and the agricultural revolution. Such recycling is not recommended nowadays. Some walls have historic value; some are archaeological evidence; some are a wildlife habitat. If it's not yours, check with the owner before moving stone, even if it looks like an abandoned pile of field clearings that have lain there for 150 years.

Choose stone carefully, as not all types are suitable for walling. Some stone discolours after it is split and exposed to the air, and some weathers badly. Check out older walls made with a particular stone to see if, or how, it has changed with time.

Beware of stone from fire-damaged sites. Granite is degraded by heat; it crumbles and is no use for a load-bearing situation. Sandstone and thin-bedded rocks become stressed by heat and liable to spalling. These are useless for walling.

Using old stone is tempting because it is weathered and covered with moss and lichens. Unfortunately, this growth will lose colour and die if the stones become part of a new wall facing south, into the open sun.

If you are lucky, the stone comes from the ground the wall is built on. Digging the foundation for a new house frequently exposes enough stone for the garden walls.

The price of stone varies from place to place, based on many factors: the cost of extraction, the distance it travelled, whether it is on a pallet or loose. In general, the more diesel that went into producing it and transporting it, the more expensive it will be.

Many types of shale and limestone are fairly soft. They cannot take the stresses of tension or compression, especially when exposed to weathering, moisture and frost. This poor-quality rock is a type of fine-grained sandstone.

Palletized Stone

Palletized rock is the modern way to go. The stone comes in regular sizes and standard thickness. It is loaded onto a truck and can be transported anywhere, at a price – the cost reflects the time taken for sorting, cleaning and packaging.

Pallets are easy to get to most sites and work from. If the budget is there, have the pallets delivered as required, for each stage of construction. This means higher costs for transporting the stone to site, but is compensated for by easier site management and convenience.

A pallet of stone usually has four good faces of reasonably laid stone in the cube, typically about 3ft (1m) high. This gives a fair idea of how much wall could be built out of one pallet.

Quarries

Quarries are an obvious source for walling stone but they generally prefer to supply large-dimensional stone or smaller material for roads and concrete production – the relatively small amounts of stone required by wallers is small beer to most quarries. They won't stockpile walling stone if it takes years to sell. The 10 tons of stone you ordered could arrive as fifteen lumps or as a load of gravel. It is best to check in with the local quarry, discuss what is needed and get a delivery of usable stone.

One good option is to hand-pick stone at a quarry (with their permission) and arrange delivery as required – the building stone should arrive first, then stone for copestones when the body of the wall is completed. This makes for easier site management.

There are advantages to hand-picking stone and knowing exactly what you are getting. Sometimes a mixed 15-ton load has all the stone you need, at a fraction of the cost of palletized stone. The downside is that the load of rough rock will need breaking, cutting and shaping, although those skills can be learned.

Repairs to an existing wall may require additional stone. A load of fresh stone mixed in with the old stone can look patchy, but there's no need to worry as new stone weathers quickly. There are lots of recipes for yogurt or dung 'tea', to speed up the process.

How Much Stone?

How much stone is required for a wall? One old maxim comes to mind: guess the amount, double it, and add 20 per cent.

A more accurate estimate, and a common reply from Scottish dykers, recommends 'a ton for every running yard of 4.5ft-high drystane dyke'. In metric terms that is one metric tonne for every linear metre of 1.4m-high wall.

Different rock types have different densities. A ton of basalt has less volume than a ton of sandstone or limestone and builds less wall than a ton of the lighter rocks.

Let us consider the volume of a yard of 4.5ft wall. A fair generalization for the weight of rock is 2.3 tons per cubic yard. The average width of the wall is assumed to be 20in. The height is 4.5ft or 54in. The length of the section is one yard or 36in.

The volume is therefore $20 \times 54 \times 36 = 38,880$cu in. Divide this by 46,656 to get 0.83cu yd. If the stone weighs 2.3 tons per cubic yard, the wall requires $2.3 \times 0.83 = 1.9$ tons per running yard.

In metric terms this is approximately equivalent to 2 metric tonnes per metre of 1.4-metre-high wall.

The calculation assumes the wall is solid, but the airspace in the tightest dry stone wall is at least 20 per cent. Allowing for this, and other variables, an attempt at an exact number takes us down a corkscrew of detail with no promise of greater accuracy. When the calculation starts getting too fussy, an informed guess could be just as accurate. The original rule of thumb from the Scottish dykers is accurate enough. It is always better to have some stone left at the end than be half a ton short. Make sure the supplier has plenty of backstock, just in case you do run out.

Any estimate should allow for breakage, loss or theft.

Choosing the Right Stones

Calculating the right amount of stone is important, but using the right kind and shape of stone is equally important. It could all come from one quarry or from different sources, depending on the wall's design.

Some of the stones in a dry stone wall have a special function and are not really interchangeable, or would be wasted if used for a lesser purpose, for example copestones, throughstones and flat foundation stones.

Working out the number of specialist stones required for a wall is fairly simple. Foundation stones are easily calculated by working out the area of the foundation – length multiplied by width. Compare that area to the average size of available stone. For throughstones, you need one every 3ft (1m), so over a 300ft (100m) wall, that would be 100. The number of coverstones is calculated by dividing the length of wall by the average width of suitable stones – those flat enough and wide enough to cover the top of the wall. To find the number of copestones, divide the total length of the wall by the average thickness of each cope.

If the stone is coming from a quarry, straight off the floor, these specialized pieces could be hand-picked by the waller. This requires some understanding between you and the quarry managers.

An ideal partnership of flat slate and round stone. Cumbria, northwest England.

Interaction with quarry machinery is usually one-sided and decisive!

Combining the numbers for the specialized stones with an estimate for face stones gives a reasonably accurate figure for the amount of stone required.

Buying smaller stone for hearting is not always necessary, as the wall produces its own hearting when stone is shaped. Less hearting is required if the build is really tight.

Don't be restricted to using one stone type in a wall – mixing different rocks creates interesting walls. This is especially satisfying if the local geology provides the stones, saving the expense of bringing them in from afar.

A contrasting mix of stone types – split boulders and local slate – make an attractive entrance to a lodge in North Ballachulish, Scotland.

Chapter Three

The Basics of Working with Stone

Health and Safety

It is not enough to assume that a workman goes on site, fit and healthy, with proper tools, and knows how to use them. Common sense safety requirements take it a bit further.

The Body

Every waller is asked about their back, and most have a story about a strain or injury that kept them off work for a week or two. Watch your back, and lift things carefully. We should all know the proper way to do it – bend the knees and keep the back straight. In the heat of the moment we can forget this, and go for a hybrid of the dead lift and upper body strength. Anyone who has worked on farms or building sites will have developed ways of lifting, using balance and experience to best advantage.

Dry stone walling is not a weightlifting competition. Most fit people are able to handle a stone up to 30lb (14kg). If it is heavy or awkward, seek assistance. Avoid lifting anything while fully extended, or on tiptoe. Lifting even a small weight under these circumstances can cause injury.

Use levers and gravity to avoid straining muscle and bone. Pinch bars are useful for moving large stones. Fair-sized stones can be moved with a wheelbarrow. Put it on its side, roll the stone into the barrow, put the barrow back on its wheels, and push it away.

Clothing and PPE

- Wear strong boots, with good soles. Steel toecaps are advisable, as stones will be dropped.
- Clothing should be up to the job, which means no lightweight linens! Wearing shorts or cut T-shirts in hot weather is an option, though it exposes skin to flying stone chips, wayward tools, grazes, bugs and sunburn. Having said that, the author recalls watching a 75-year-old waller in Mallorca, working from a very basic scaffold, clad only in shorts and tennis shoes. His stonework was exemplary.
- Waterproofs are essential in some climates, whatever the season.
- Wearing a hard hat is sometimes a good idea.
- Protect your eyes; stone chips, even a dry grass stalk, can cause injury, and pain – a lot of pain. Safety glasses are light and cheap; there is no need for cumbersome goggles.
- Wear good-quality gloves unless your hands are used to manual work, but make sure the gloves are thin enough for you to still feel the stone; don't use thick leather or welders' gloves, which are unwieldy and will get in the way. Gloves are especially recommended for dismantling old walls. There's a remarkable amount of broken glass and metal in there. One reasonable alternative to gloves is electricians' tape, wrapped round the thumb and forefingers.

The Site

- Always be aware of what is happening around you. Don't walk backwards while carrying weight. Be aware how your movements affect others and how their actions might affect you.
- Keep a clear space, a couple of feet wide, at the base of the wall. This safe corridor reduces the trip hazard. It also looks more professional and separates the organized scene of a build in progress from the confusion of the raw material.
- Keep the site as compact as possible and as tidy as possible. Don't throw stone far from where you need it. You will lift the equivalent of several tons of stone in a day; there's no need to walk miles to carry it.
- Cover the end of projecting pins, posts or scaffolding with some sort of padding or high-viz tape.
- If a wall encloses livestock, don't leave a gap for the animals to get out when the site is left overnight. Don't throw stone onto grassland, where it may damage farm equipment or an animal's feet.
- Be aware of what is on, above and under the site. Before starting work, check for buried electric cables, drains and so on.
- In some countries there might be a hazard under every stone. Lift stones carefully to give any biting, stinging or spitting beastie a chance to get away.
- Working by the sides of the road is risky, and traffic cones and red tape might not be enough. In some situations, the local authority may insist on traffic management systems, which will add considerably to cost.

Just in Case

- Check that you have phone reception and know where medical services are.
- Have a first-aid kit on site, and make sure everyone has some idea of how to use it – the person with the first-aid qualification may be the one who gets injured.
- It is worth doing a risk assessment for each new site. Standard format forms are available online at www.hse.gov.uk. Be realistic; 'health and safety' often has a bad reputation, mostly because of over-zealous interpretation of sensible regulations. Completing one of the forms does get you thinking about the site, and a safe site is an efficient site.
- Remember – in the event of injury, loss or damage, the insurance company has the final say.

Tools

The dry stone waller does not need many specialized tools to build a new wall or repair an old one.

In classic agricultural dry stone walling, the stone was, and is, used with a minimum of shaping. The wallers picked up the stone, and, after several instinctive decisions, placed it. They went to a site with little more than a couple of hammers, string lines and some digging tools.

Modern dry stone walling, covered in Chapter 11, has more sophisticated tools. Greater accuracy is required for some of these projects and less time is spent on laborious manual shaping.

The circumstances of the work site dictate what machinery can be used. Consider the limitations forced by narrow gates, passageways, trees and underground services before committing to a design. One particular site may be ideal for a Bobcat and excavator; the layout of another might limit equipment to a wheelbarrow and spade.

Scaffolding is not normally required for dry stone walling, although it may be useful for taller structures to limit the amount of lifting and stretching.

A Simple Set of Tools

- A spade will cut the foundation, but it need not be extensive – clear a shallow trench down to firm ground.
- The pinch bar (on the right) helps move large stones and dig into the ground.
- The 8lb (3.6kg) sledgehammer, 4lb (1.8kg) mason's hammer and 22oz (600g) brick hammer are sufficient to break up most sizes of rock and shape it. It is worth investing in good hammers.
- A spirit level and tape measure help keep measurements accurate and consistent. The first few feet of a sprung tape measure are normally all that is used on a wall. A cloth tape on a reel is more accurate for longer distances.
- A pointed chisel is useful for knocking off bumps and knobbles. A wide range of chisels is available for cutting stone, but they are best left for use by the experienced mason who demands tighter joints. The chisel options, and how to use them, will petrify the novice.
- A two-handled plastic bucket is useful for carrying hearting and moving stone and earth. At the end of the day, it also carries the tools home.

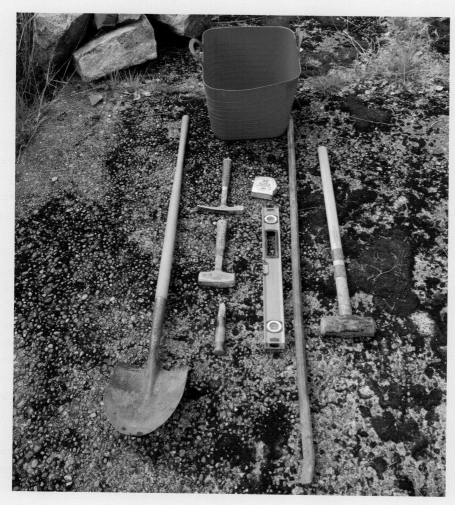

This selection of tools is enough to start with. Red tape around the handles makes them more difficult to lose and confirms ownership.

Breaking Stone

Walling is not about breaking rock; it is more about putting stone together. Wallers and dykers learned to use their local stone with a minimum of cutting or trimming. If the rock was broken down by nature into oblong blocks, that's how it was used. On the other hand, if the rock type appeared as flat slabs then that was used, equally efficiently, to create a wall. The design detail of a wall depends on the available stone, as we shall see later from images of walls from Scotland, Ireland, England and further afield.

As a generalization – a very general one – all the stones in a pile will have the same shape and angle, though they are different sizes. With experience, the waller learns how to put these together. For example, two 45-degree angles fit perfectly together if one piece is upside down. Two thin pieces, on top of each other, often match the height of a thick piece.

Some of the stones will need shaping to fit the scale of the wall, or a particular place in the wall. Foundation stones should be relatively flat and fit tightly together. This creates as big a footprint as possible on the ground and provides a broad base for the stones sitting on top. Throughstones are ideal as long narrow shapes, while coverstones should be broad, flat and thin. The ideal vertical copestones are slim pieces with a flat base.

Caution! Breaking a stone takes time and effort and may not achieve the desired result. Some large stones are best kept for special purposes. It is relatively easy to break a large stone but much more difficult to recreate its potential from a pile of small rubble.

Stonebreaking Tools

Tools for shaping stone need not be expensive or specialized. Choose tools made for the job; it is a bit jarring to see a carpenter's hammer used for stonework (though having said that, it would be a useful tool for trimming thin stone). Lighter tools take care of sandstones and limestones but heavier tools are required for granites and basalts.

A 10lb (4.5kg) or an 8lb (3.6kg) sledgehammer will break down most large rocks. A 4lb (1.8kg) mason's hammer and a 3lb (1.4kg) club hammer will take care of the rough shaping, and a 22oz (600g) brick hammer will deal with the final trimming. 'Brick hammer' is a generic name for a tool used in all stone and brick trades. It has one rectangular or square face and one chisel-shaped face.

A pointed chisel is useful for taking off high spots. A 0.75in (19mm) flat chisel will take down ridges or extended high points.

There are many types of chisel, meant for different types of stone, including steel chisels and the more durable carbide-tipped ones. Start off with a good steel chisel and upgrade it when you get more experienced – carbide-tipped tools are tough but delicate. More than one has been ruined when it was thrown into a bucket of tools and the carbide tip crashed into a hammer head.

Breaking Different Rock Types

It is possible to break a large piece of rock by hitting it in the middle with a big hammer. There is no control, and it usually produces four (or five) irregular quarters. Applying a bit of finesse to the process may help get a few useful stones out of a large rock.

You are probably familiar with the 'magic' process of splitting stones with pins and feathers, also known as wedges and shims. A series of holes are drilled a few inches apart. Two shims of metal (feathers) are set into each hole and a wedge or pin is slid between them. The wedges are tapped into the holes, sliding down the feathers, exerting pressure on the stone until eventually it splits. That's the ultimate in stone breaking – boulders weighing many tons are split this way.

A large piece of stone will break if it is struck several times, in a line, across its width – a more brutal version of splitting with pins and feathers. A finer way of doing this is with a tracer chisel, which is a chisel specifically made for splitting stone. The underlying principle for all these methods is to apply a line of force down into the stone, and repeat it until a stress line becomes a fracture.

Sedimentary rocks, shales, slates and sandstones, will break more easily along a bedding plane. Those are usually clearly visible as a line in the sedimentary beds. Wallers who use a particular stone every day learn to recognize sequences of colouring that indicate where it will break. Generally speaking, find a dark line (indicating a flaw line with moisture in it), and use a hammer, or hammer and chisel, to open that up.

For thin-bedded stone, the chisel-faced end of a brick hammer is as handy to use as an actual chisel, and quicker, depending on how fine a cut you want. Give the stone time to split. If the hit is too heavy, and repeated too quickly, the stone may shatter before it eases apart.

Metamorphic rocks often have horizontal bedding planes and vertical cracks, depending on how they were created. Hammering along these fault lines is enough to split them.

Boulders appear intimidating; they need not be. They are pieces of bedrock, broken off and rounded by glacier ice and water, but they still behave like the parent rock. A few hits across their width is enough to snap them in two. If they were born as sandstones, a series of well-placed hits along one side will usually break them into flatter pieces.

Shaping stone before starting to build has its advantages. Wallers in Mallorca receive stone on site as rough boulders and spend time preparing each stone to a standard shape, but not to a standard size, before using any of it. This ensures maximum stone-on-stone contact, and speeds up the build process.

Don't break a stone while it is sitting on the wall. Do any shaping and hammering on the ground, or on top of another stone, using it as an anvil. A wall may be strong but it won't take short, sharp impacts from a hammer blow.

If you are shaping, you are not walling. Settle for a happy medium of making the stone fit; if you are too fussy and then end up dropping the standard, it will affect the appearance of the wall.

Breaking and trimming stone is best learned on a work site or on a training course. The mistakes can be used to fill the inside of the wall!

Saws and grinders are useful for precision cuts and preparation of level surfaces. Modern tools do save time, though bear in mind that none of them existed when York Minster was built.

This is a very general introduction to breaking stone. Chapter 4 discusses the trimming of individual stones so they fit into the face of the wall, which requires a more precise way of cutting than that for splitting or breaking large stones.

Establishing the Dimensions

The A-Frame

The shape of the A-frame represents the profile of the wall. *See* box. It creates a straight edge from which to stretch a string line to another straight edge. This sets the outer edge of each course of stone in the face of the wall and, as the lines are raised (after each course is completed), the upper edge of each course.

The width of the frame reduces with height. This represents the batter of the wall, a feature of most free-standing dry stone walls. This tapering adds to strength and stability. The batter also indicates what size of stone is laid where. The larger stones sit in, or near, the bottom of the wall, where there is most room for them. Stones normally decrease in size towards the top of the wall, up to where it is narrowest.

Using a frame with a solid edge makes sure the dimensions are consistent. Measurement decisions are made once – when the frame is screwed together. Crossbars in the frame can indicate the height of the throughstone and the coverband, forming a permanent indication for the siting of these important stones. There is no need to constantly remeasure or recalculate their position.

The A-Frame

This frame is set up for a fairly typical dry stone wall. The width at the bottom, from outer edge to outer edge of the timber, is 28in (71cm), representing the width of the foundation.

The underside of the lower crossbar indicates the height of the throughstone. The bottom edge of the top crossbar represents the top of the double, below the copestones. At that point the measurement from outer edge to outer edge is 14in (36cm).

The timber is fixed so that it slopes evenly between the width of the foundation and the width below the copestones. This defines the batter for each side of the wall.

Lines are used with A-frames to define the profile of the wall over its length. Spring clamps are a convenient way of attaching the lines to the frame.

This frame assumes the same batter on each side of the wall, but the design can be adjusted to suit any shape of wall.

A typical A-frame with two sets of lines, wound onto steel pins. A minimum of two frames is required to start a new wall.

Generally speaking, higher walls mean wider foundations. As a rule of thumb, the width of the wall under the copestones is reckoned to be half the width of the foundation. Those two measurements, added together, are said to represent the height of the wall before the copestones are added. This is a very rough guide, however, and there are many variations, depending on the purpose of the wall and the rock type.

The generalization can also be unwieldy. If we use it to calculate the dimensions of a dry stone wall with a width of 15in (38cm) under the copestones (about as narrow as it can be) and a height of 5ft or 60in (152cm) to below the copestones, we get a foundation width of 45in (60–15 = 45), or 114cm. That would use a lot of stone and increase the building time. In practice this wall would be built slimmer and tighter, perhaps with more throughstones for added strength.

When building a new wall with a local stone, take a look around to see what previous generations of wallers did, and replicate that. They will have used the stone in the most efficient way.

The A-frame is the master guide for the build. Once the dimensions of the wall are decided, build two or three frames to that size. The measurements could be to the inside or the outside edge of the timber; just be consistent with the design and how they are used. The frames for a particular project should all be the same, and interchangeable. If three or more frames are to be used over a length of new build, have the measurements to the inside of the timber. This makes sure the wood does not get in the way as you lay stones along the string line.

The Batter

The angle or slope indicated by the edge of the A-frame is the batter of the wall. A wall's batter (also described as its camber) is its narrowing or tapering with height, and is a way of adding strength to the structure. A battered wall has the weight of the wall securely centred above its base, so is unlikely to topple over. A typical batter might be one in six, meaning that the wall's width decreases by 1in (usually on each side) for every 6in rise in height (2.5cm for every 15cm), approximately 10 per cent.

The batter is normally the same on both sides of the wall but there is nothing to stop a wall having a different batter on each side. Garden walls look better with a near-vertical, very steep batter, so a good design for a tall garden wall might have a one in six batter on the outside and a vertical face on the inside. The steeper inside face provides an ideal surface for growing plants against, like peaches or climbing roses. The batter on the outside face means the wall is narrowing towards the top and uses less stone in its construction.

There is such a thing as 'negative batter' – when the width of the wall increases with height. This creates an overhang, which would be useful if the wall is needed, say, to contain or keep out clambering animals. It also offers some interesting design opportunities.

The batter might be steeper with some types of rock and shallower with others. Large stones often mean walls with less batter and, contradictorily, small stones sometimes also produce walls with less batter. It very much depends on the local stone and how the wallers work it.

Setting the Frames

When building a length of straight wall, a frame is set, level and plumb, at one end of the section, held there by a vertical post or reinforcing bar, maybe a foot away from the end of the wall to give space for the construction of a wall end. Another frame is fixed at the far end of the section. String lines are stretched tight between the frames. The lines represent the edges of construction. It is the upper and outer edge for a course of stone.

For short sections, easily completed in a day by one or two persons, two frames are sufficient to start a new wall. After the first section is completed, only one frame is needed. It is set a few yards further on and

A section of racked back wall, the temporary end of an ongoing rebuild. An A-frame (now removed) guided the repair to this point. We see the face stones reaching well into the centre of the wall and the throughstone spanning the wall. The hearting is also clearly visible. For the next stretch of the wall, a frame is set up a few metres further on. String lines are stretched between this built section (which now expresses the dimensions of the wall) and the frame. The batter of the wall can be clearly seen.

the completed section, racked back, or raked back, becomes the profile for one end. Working from such an inclined end gives a smoother transition between sections. Building a vertical, or near-vertical end, is extra work and means a rougher transition.

For longer sections, or where the ground rises and falls, three or more frames may be useful. As mentioned above, if you decide to put set several frames along a section, adapt the design of the A-frame to make sure the measurements are taken to the inside of the timber to make it easier to build through the middle frames.

When using three or more frames in a stretch, take care to avoid running joints behind the intermediate frames. This fault is detailed in Chapter 5. It is a tricky spot to reach and, if left to last, is usually filled with a fussy piece of stone. Take care to ensure joints are properly broken behind the frames by laying a stone behind these uprights first, then work to either side of it.

Frames get in the way when repairing a collapsed section of wall, unless it is a long stretch. In this case, instead of a frame, the lines are usually stretched on pins inserted between the stones on either end of the gap. Posts or lengths of rebar, laid against the standing wall, are ideal substitutes for a frame.

Using Lines

This section uses the terms 'line', 'lines' and 'string lines' interchangeably. It should be clear from the text whether the term refers to a string line (used as a guide to guarantee straight-edge construction), or to the line of the wall – the way the wall proceeds through the landscape, whether it is curved or straight.

Using a string line helps keep individual stones, and whole courses (layers of stone), straight, level and square. After one course of stone is properly laid, it becomes a reliable support for the course above it. If a flat stone is laid at a tilt, it is difficult to build on top of, and it disturbs the horizontal pattern.

String lines come in many types and qualities. The best ones are braided synthetics, as they last longer and are less likely to tangle. Choose a highly visible colour.

The lines are easily wound onto steel pins with flattened ends. These pins are simply pushed into gaps between the stonework or wrapped around the frame. Spring clamps are a convenient way to hold lines on to the frame; there are no knots to manipulate in wet or muddy conditions.

This wall, among other faults, includes several badly laid flat stones, with repercussions in the upper courses. Spaces are filled with random chinking. Minor attention with a hammer, or levelling up with thinner pieces, would have created a level, tighter build.

The string line is stretched, tightly, between the straight edges of two frames to define the face of the wall. The line is set with the aid of a spirit level to make sure it is truly horizontal.

When a stone is laid on a wall, it should come within a fraction of an inch of the line, without actually touching. When laying stone, take care not to push the line out. If the nose of one stone pushes the string line out by an inch this causes a skew in the work, possibly for several courses until the error is spotted and corrected.

Good line discipline creates a uniform batter from top to bottom with no bulges or indents, and a straight wall where it should be straight.

The lines on both sides of the wall are raised after every course is completed. Raise them by the average thickness of the stone and check the lines are level, end to end and side to side, with a spirit level. This is especially important if the aim is to go for strict coursing.

The author's preference is to use one line on each side of the frame. This method is especially effective where only one or two people are working on a section and keeping pace with each other.

Others prefer using two lines on each side, one at the foundation and one higher up at, say, throughstone height. By sighting from one line down to the other while placing the stone, the waller is able to lay the stone accurately with the correct batter. This method is useful on longer sections if several people are working on each side, and some are faster than others.

Some wallers set multiple lines – at foundation, throughstones, top of double and top of cope. This may have advantages but it creates a web of string that is difficult to work through, especially if there are several people on a section.

When lines are tied to a wooden frame, it is important to tie them consistently to the same side of the wood. The difference in width might be an inch or as much as 4in (10cm) – enough to cause a skew or bulge in the work.

If the new wall is long, say over 100 yards or metres, it is a good idea to set pegs along the route of the wall to establish a straight master line. Start construction from one end, and work in short stretches that can be completed in one or two days. On completion of each short section, move the frame along the master line a few yards and reset the string lines between the racked back section of the completed wall and the frame.

When repairing a gap, stretch the string lines between the standing stonework at each end of the collapse. The profile and heights are taken from there, even if the wall has swayed or widened a little. There is no need to make extra work by taking down the wall until it gets to an ideal profile.

Setting Lines for Pillars and Curved Shapes

A framework or a long enough vertical pin and a piece of string are all that is required to make the outline for shapes with a straight or curved edge. Once the outer limits of the stonework are defined, the stone can be selected, or shaped, to suit.

A Square Pillar

This method, shown in the image, can be modified for any size of pillar or any straight-sided shape.

The top plate is fixed on to the vertical steel pole. It becomes the central core of the pillar and the channel for a power cable. The four vertical lines are the four corners of the pillar. They fall from holes in the top plate and are fixed into the concrete foundation by screws – after checking with spirit level and tape that they are level and square in all directions. Once the lines are set, the guesswork is taken out of the stone-laying process.

Start work by laying right-angled stones in each corner. Their edges should correspond to a straight line between vertical strings. Lay smaller stones between. Check constantly to make sure the courses are level and, with a long straight edge between the lines, make sure the faces of the pillar are straight and vertical.

These lines are set up for a square pillar.

The lines must be checked often, to make sure they have not been disturbed. Some lines loosen if they get wet and tighten if they dry.

The pillar shown here was built using all the principles of dry work though it was mortared. The mortar was held back from the stones' edges and was mostly invisible. The pillar supported a gate at an estate entrance, and the metalwork welded on the right of the vertical post eventually formed the hinges.

Pyramids, Round Pillars and Cones

The arrangement of lines for a square pillar described above is easily adapted for a pillar of any size with flat edges. For a pillar with sloping edges, simply adjust the measurements on the top plate and down where the lines meet the foundation.

This arrangement can also be used for a three- or four-sided pyramid. In that case, all the lines would be set from the one point on a vertical central pin, representing the height of the pyramid. The lines are angled down to the foundation and fixed. The central pin is then sacrificed as a reinforcement.

For a solid round pillar, a central pin (thick rebar is ideal) is set vertically, and a trammel – a piece of wire or string, half the length of the intended diameter – is used to indicate the outer edge of the stonework. Stones are laid to the limit of that string, course by course.

If the pillar is the same diameter all the way to the top, the string will always be the same length. If it narrows towards the top, the string would be shortened slightly with each course of stone. It would be a good idea to regulate this by drawing a plan that defines how the trammel shortens with height. This arrangement could also guide the building of a round shape.

Any pillar, round or square, benefits from a capstone. The cap could be a single piece of stone or a carefully designed arrangement of smaller pieces. It is a good idea to check what is available for use as a cap before starting, and, if necessary, consider altering the design of the pillar to suit the available cap.

A Half-Round Plinth or Pillar

One line and three vertical lengths of rebar are all that is necessary to create the outline for a half-round pillar or plinth. Set the three verticals in a straight line. The two outer verticals mark the outer edges of the pillar, and the third vertical is set in the middle. The straight line between the three uprights indicates the flat front edge. A piece of string, long enough to stretch from the central vertical to each of the outer two, pivots round to indicate the curved back edge of the plinth. If stones are laid to the back curved edge and the front straight edge, the shape will emerge as the courses rise – much like a 3D printer puts layer on top of layer to create a three-dimensional 'thing'. The size of the plinth can be varied by moving the verticals nearer or further apart. The uprights should be as tall as the intended height of the plinth. A spirit level will be useful to keep the string and the coursing relatively level.

How Much to Build at a Time?

Readers are recommended to watch *Triumph of the Wall*, a 2013 documentary film directed by Bill Stone, starring Bill Stone and Chris Overing. It describes how a 1,000ft (300m) wall, scheduled to take eight weeks, took eight years to complete. The film concentrates on the daily grind of stonework as the novice wallers resolve many issues and eventually complete the wall, and themselves.

Some viewers will be frustrated, perhaps reduced to deep despair, when they see how the wall is built. Long sections of foundation are laid out; the long section is fully completed; then the wallers move on to another long section.

This is disheartening. If you have such a project, break it down to manageable chunks. Instead of setting up two weeks' work, lay the foundation for a day's work, maybe two, and work until that section is finished. This progress is more encouraging. Every day or two another piece of wall is totally completed. If there are

The flat front face of a half-round pillar, approximately 2.5ft (75cm) high at the front, 3ft (90cm) at the back. Three vertical sections of rebar were set along a straight edge. Two marked the outer edge of the plinth, and the third, set in the middle, was the pivot point for the string line.

A side view of the half-round pillar. The flat front was constantly checked to ensure a straight edge between the three pins. There is a slight batter to the plinth. That was judged by eye, as was the way the stonework curved into the information panel. The mortar in this plinth was kept back from the face of the stones so it has the appearance of being built dry.

imperfections in any section of the build, the waller immediately sees them and can strive to improve the techniques in the next day's work. Working on shorter sections provides more variety than working on one 50-yard course of stone that takes days to complete.

On the other hand, your personal psyche might favour doing long stints at a time, and accept the delayed gratification of seeing long sections totally completed.

The stretches can be longer if there are several wallers on site. Working in pairs is better than working alone, unless one is the stereotypical curmudgeon. If one person works on each side, it provides company and keeps the pace up. Also, being separated by the wall, they don't get in each other's way and are not competing for stone. This way of working also keeps the stonework consistent. Different wallers have different signature styles, even with the same stone on the same site.

When working from a jumbled load of stone, it is a good plan to haul out the 'ugly' stones while sorting the pile. Use these stones to lay out a long section of foundation to get them out of the way. After that, set up shorter sections that can be completed in a day or two. The A-frames will easily straddle the foundation stones as each, shorter, section is built.

Chapter Four

Laying, Trimming and Securing Stone

The Essential Principles for Laying Stone

These walls use no mortar: gravity and friction are the only adhesive, and proper placement is the only glue. John Shaw-Rimmington, a well know Canadian waller and stonemason, summed it up when asked 'What kind of cement do you use?' He replied 'It's called gravity. It's better than any manufactured product I've tried. You can get it almost anywhere. It's not expensive. And it lasts forever.'

A sign at the Marenakos stone yard, near Seattle, confirms 'Mortar is not a glue; gravity is your friend.'

Refresher: Single and Double Walls

The following sections makes frequent references to single and double walls. Here is a quick revision of the differences between the two.

A single wall, or dyke, is one stone wide. The largest stones are set in the bottom course with smaller stones on each succeeding course, up to a level top.

In a double wall, two outer faces of tightly built face stones are stabilized by hearting in the middle.

Occasional long stones (throughstones) are laid across the width of the wall to connect both faces to add strength and stability. The wall is topped off with a layer of flat coverstones and the copestones.

A single wall built from glacial boulders. The largest spaces between the boulders are chocked with smaller stones. Lairg, Scotland.

This cross-section of a typical Scottish double dyke exposes the various components. The dark space below the throughstone suggests a lack of hearting.

Rules – Guidance for the Wise

The following recommendations, well tried and tested, produce the best work for a double wall. They also apply when building single walls, though less rigorously, reflecting the more open nature of the stonework.

1. Lay individual stones flat and level, with their longest edge into the centre of the wall, at least one-third of the way across the wall.
2. Never lay stones with their longest edge along the face of the wall. This is called traced walling and is generally regarded as a weak way to build. This topic is covered in more detail below.
3. Lay stones tightly together with as much side-to-side contact as possible. They should, at the very minimum, fit tightly together at the face of the wall, and for several inches into the wall.
4. Fill any spaces between stones or under stones, carefully, with hearting to jam the larger stones in place and eliminate movement in any direction. Place the hearting immediately after placing the face stone.
5. Stones in any course should lie across the joint between the two stones below it, with as much direct contact between stones as possible – the well-known 'one over two, two over one' rule. This is more fully described below under Breaking the Joint.
6. After laying a few stones, take a step back and look at the work. If you are not totally satisfied, take it down and start again.
7. Work to the line – up to the line and out to the line. This goes a long way to forming a level base for the next course. There's no great harm in occasionally going above the line with an individual stone, but never push the line out with a badly laid face stone. Check the line constantly.
8. Raise the line by the average thickness of the stones after completing each course.

These recommendations are not all set in stone. An experienced waller knows when to break rules and how to compensate for the lapse. Any one of these recommendations could be broken on an individual occasion, even multiple occasions, and still produce a strong wall. More care is required to produce an attractive wall, however – that requires attention to detail.

These rules are easily applied to flat stone with parallel edges, but can also be made to work for irregular material. We shall see in Chapter 5 how the basic principles apply to a wide range of stone types, from thin shale to round stones and large slabs.

Breaking the Joint

One essential principle in any stonework is breaking the joint. It is essential for a good, strong bonding pattern, with maximum contact between the stones. Anyone who has played with wooden blocks, or the plastic interlocking type, understands the need to create strength with a dovetailing pattern of interlinking pieces. Proper bonding spreads the load down to the foundation and reduces the chance of asymmetrical pressures causing collapse.

If a joint between two stones is not covered by the stone on the next course, and that is repeated up into the third course, this is called a running joint, and is usually betrayed by a vertical dark line. This immediately suggests bad bonding and begs further investigation. A 'zipper joint' is a series of almost, but not quite broken joints up through several courses, which resembles a zip in clothing. The overlaps are there but maybe only an inch, where they should be three or four.

Floaters and Riders

Following the principle of breaking the joint is easy when using flat stone in a combination of standard

Stacked, Not Bonded

This retaining wall has several running joints, visible as dark vertical lines. The most obvious of these are caused by large pieces butting up against each other. The largest stones, including the block in the middle, would be better used in the foundation. The others could then be laid in a stronger, mixed, pattern, with two small stones lying against a larger one, and one laid over the top, following the 'one over two, two over one' rule.

A stream of running joints. It is the lack of symmetry and balance, as much as anything, that upsets the eye.

sizes, but becomes a little more difficult when using small or rough irregular stone. In practice, not every joint is broken by the stone immediately above it. Sometimes one large stone must lie across the top of three or more smaller ones. This is sometimes described as 'one over three'. Extra care is essential in this situation to make sure all the small stones are securely held by the larger ones.

Traced Stone and Stone on Edge

Do not be tempted to lay a stone with its longest edge along the length of the wall, unless it reaches at least a third of the way into the centre. Laying narrow stones with their length along the wall (traced walling) is begging for trouble. It is structurally weak because the stone is more easily pushed over the edge.

An ornamental interior wall with several examples of running joints, and some well-covered joints. The small stones on their edge must have been inserted later. This suggests the wall moved some time during construction.

This wall contains several vertical running joints and diagonal 'zipper joints'. This is not a strong wall. Taking extra care when placing stone and thinking ahead would have avoided this unsightly work.

A good mix of small and larger stone, with many examples of 'one-over-three'. Experienced wallers have made sure the build is tight. Dry Stone Walling Association collection, Cumbria, England.

The thin flat stone (third from top) is what is known as a 'rider'; it seems to 'float' above the orange stone in the centre. In fact, the orange stone was tightly held inside the wall. A little shaping with a light hammer would have fitted several of these stones more tightly together.

The two stones in the middle are laid traced, with their longest edge along the wall. The centre is full of loose hearting. The builder missed an opportunity for good solid building and creating maximum friction between horizontal and vertical stones.

A traced stone is also more likely to sit across the top of three or four below it, and less likely to hold them all securely in place.

The wall is stronger if the stones are laid with their longest edges into the centre of the wall, so the inner end of the stone is held in place by the weight above it and there is far less chance of it moving. This gives more 'length-in strength', more internal contact between large stones and a reasonable amount of hearting. It is obviously better to fill a space with

A good arrangement of stones. They all reach well into the centre of the wall, with a lot less loose hearting. Minor attention with a hammer was all that was necessary to make these stones fit better together.

This wall was rebuilt when a main road was realigned. The work is poor, and parts collapsed within months of completion. A view along the wall proves stone had been laid traced and on edge. This gives best value for face area of stone but is structurally weak. The hearting is rounded stone, most likely from a beach. The collapse was caused by poorly placed stones moving because of the pressure put on them by the cope.

good building stone and some hearting to secure it, rather than poorly laid stone backed up with a lot of small stone infill.

Some stone types – shales, slate and thin flagstones – are often laid with a long edge along the wall. This is still a strong way to build if another long edge of the stone reaches at least a third, preferably half, of the way into the centre of the wall and is securely held by the stones around it.

Sometimes a stone is laid traced because there is no other option. If that happens, the stone, or stones, on top must be laid with their length into the wall to solidly connect the traced stone with the interior of the wall and restore stability. This is a classic situation where the experienced waller knows what to do to get over a little temporary difficulty and still produce strong work. The novice should try not to get into that corner in the first place.

Shiners, Soldiers and Sailors

An individual stone laid vertically within a course of horizontal stones looks odd – it catches the eye. In random work, with irregular stone, one set on edge is not so obvious. Sometimes the only stone that will fit into a space is a small piece that must be set vertically. This is often the result of poor stone choice. Set stone tight against stone, and try not to leave small spaces that need specifically sized stones to fill the gap.

In dry stone terminology, these irregulars are called 'shiners'. Shiners can be 'soldiers' or 'sailors', depending on whether they show an edge or a broad face to the outside. This is brick terminology which has leaked into stonework.

These vertical stones are best avoided because, to the critical eye, they suggest something is wrong. A vertical stone is not sitting on its most stable edge, but it can be as strong as a horizontally laid stone so long as it is gripped by all the stones around it and reaches well into the wall. The worst shiner would be a short piece of stone sitting loosely in a space, contributing nothing to the structural strength.

Vertically laid stones can actually add visual interest if they are set as a regular pattern.

Trimming Stone

When laying stone, don't worry too much about slight bumps and hollows on the top or bottom of a stone, as the other stones will have corresponding irregularities. Any small nibs are easily snipped off with a brick hammer or a pointed chisel. That is usually enough to increase the contact area between stones.

Should the flattest surface of the stone go up or down? The answer is to lay stones in whatever way gets the maximum contact between them and provides the best bed for the next course.

It is equally important to pay attention to the front of the stone – the edge that becomes part of the face of the wall. It may need trimming to fit into the horizontal and vertical profile of the wall.

Projecting stone edges should be chipped or nibbled off in small pieces. Chip across the projection, not into it. Use a larger stone as an anvil. This gives more control over the shaping process.

Facing up to the Batter

This diagram represents a cut through a dry stone wall, showing different-shaped stones and how they correspond to the batter. Some stones are not laid well. The slanted line represents the batter of the wall, and, at any point, represents the horizontal string line stretched between two A-frames. The following discrepancies are easily rectified as the build proceeds but are more difficult to correct after the wall is completed:

Stone A slopes downwards towards the outer edge of the wall. It is difficult, though not impossible, to build on. If the stone was high on the outer face and sloped down towards the middle of the wall, that would be a definite improvement.

Stone B appears to be ideal. Its face lies a fraction of an inch from a horizontal string line and corresponds with the batter of the wall.

Stone C is laid upside down. Its face lies contrary to the line of batter. In this instance, though it is not structurally weak, it does catch the eye and is best corrected. The face of the stone could be trimmed to bring it in line with the batter, or the stone could be laid the other way up.

Stone D has been pinned up on the inside of the wall to bring its face into line with the batter of the wall; one solid pinning does the job. It has been used correctly, from the inside of the wall, and will never move. A gathering of smaller pieces would increase the chance of movement if they crush together. This stone could be the other way up, with the angled inner face (seen above the pinning), on the top side. This would also create maximum contact between stones E and D, once E is adjusted.

Stone E has one edge in line with the batter, but the face slopes sharply back. If the bottom edge is trimmed to square off the face, the stone can be moved closer to the face of the wall. It will then be totally in line with the batter and provide more support for stone D. When a stone is properly laid, it becomes a secure base for stone in the upper courses.

Stone F looks satisfactory but the front pinning under it deserves investigation. It may be there because it supports the larger stone, or it may simply be decoration to fill a hole. Pinnings in the front of a wall must be secure, unlikely to move or break. It is better to leave a small space empty than insert a small stone that will trickle out. If a smaller stone must be used on the face of the wall, perhaps to bring a larger one up to a height, it should reach well into the wall and be securely held by all the stones around it. It must be laid in the course of construction, not added later as an afterthought.

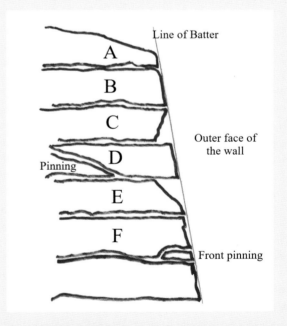

Cross-section of a wall, showing various shapes of face stone in relation to the batter line.

Stepped Walling

Some granite walls are built out of thick blocks. Let us imagine a 4ft-high (1.2m) wall made out of 6in-thick (15cm) stones. Six stones on top of each other make up the height of the body of the wall, and there would normally be a 12in (30cm) vertical cope on top of that.

The blocks could have a natural face that corresponds with the batter, but more likely they will need trimming to suit. This means extra time and labour. For this reason, walls built out of thick stone, or hard, difficult-to-work rock types, often have little or no batter. Trying to force blocky stone into a one-in-six batter takes more work than trying to produce a one-in-ten batter with the same stone – assuming the same height of wall.

Referring to the diagram, stones D and E are set with their bottom edges correct in their relationship with the horizontal string line, but their top edges need trimming to bring the whole face of the stones into line with the batter of the wall.

Stones B and C were laid with their top edge correct to the line. The top edge of these stones needs trimming back, so the bottom edge can be brought forward. The face of the stones will then correspond to the batter of the wall.

The three thin stones at the top (marked A) correspond to the batter. Thinner stones are easier to shape than thick stones and do not always need trimming. The stepped effect of three thin stones laid to the batter is less eye-catching. Making a 6in (15cm) rise over that batter with three thin stones is easier than getting to the batter with one 6in (15cm) stone.

The bottom stone is a scarcement for the wall. The scarcement projects from the wall for its total length; it is an intentional part of the structure.

Stepped walling is a result of bad work or lack of attention to detail; it might be a short series of stones or an entire course. Avoid it by working carefully to the line and making sure the face of each stone corresponds to the batter of the wall.

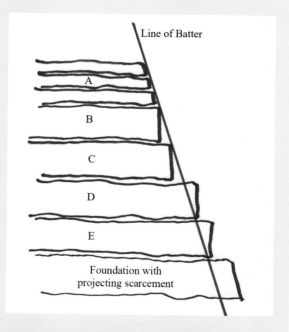

A cross-section of a wall showing stepped walling and a scarcement. The slanted line represents the batter of the wall and, at any point, the horizontal string line, stretched between two A-frames. The thick stones have a jagged relationship with the batter of the wall. The wall looks stepped, like a staircase.

Hearting, Fill and Packing

In most instances, stones don't fit tightly together. The void space in a wall, even after the most careful hearting, is reckoned to be 20–24 per cent. These spaces must be filled with smaller stones to reduce the chance of the larger stones moving. These small stones, known as hearting, fill, shims, wedges or packing, are the smallest component in a dry stone wall but have big responsibilities. Properly placed hearting increases friction – the 'glue' that holds walls together.

A lot of hearting stone is produced during the building process, when stones are trimmed. The interior of many of those old dry stone walls, crossing moor and glen, are full of spalls broken off rough boulders.

If hearting has to be imported, get 2–4in (5–10cm) angular crushed rock. Use hard stone, not shales or types that will break down with weathering. Never use gravel or a mix of chips, soil and grass swept from the ground. This rubbish adds no structural strength and melts in the rain. Rounded stone is also unsuitable. It acts like ball bearings, providing an opportunity for smooth transmission of stresses and pressures. This reduces friction and allows larger stones to move and take others with them.

Hearting must be placed carefully, by hand, an automatic action immediately after setting each face stone. At that point the spaces between the stones are easy to see and easy to get at. Never, ever, pour it in from a bucket and leave it to find its own level. At a pinch, it is acceptable to put a small pile of hearting in the middle of the wall, if it is then carefully redistributed by hand.

This dyke shows a lack of hearting. Maybe it was never put there, or else it slipped down into the body of the dyke as it flexed and settled.

If a wall proceeds up through several courses without proper hearting or interlinking between the face stones, that is called 'tower building', and is akin to piling wooden blocks in the nursery. This type of walling has very little structural strength and will fail. Leaving hearting 'until later' means the wall fails sooner.

Hearting should fit snugly. Never force it into a space or tap it between stones with a hammer. That is likely to push stones apart, once more reducing the effects of friction.

Keep the middle of the wall well filled, even slightly higher, than the face stones, before moving up to the next course. Constantly levelling out the hearting with the outer stones like this makes sure no space is missed, and makes it easier on the eye when considering how to place a stone on the wall.

Face stones can be supported, or brought into line, by placing shims or wedges under the tail end inside the wall. These critical spaces should, ideally, be filled with one piece of stone. One supporting piece is better than a collection of smaller pieces, and is certainly preferable to a handful of small chips carelessly thrown in. When weight presses down on these chips, they will try to crush down into a smaller volume, thus creating space, which eventually leads to movement.

The interior of a wall is beyond inspection after the wall is completed. Scrimping on the hearting and internal pinning was one way of speeding up the building process. The original chroniclers of dry stone walling were particularly insistent that hearting be done properly, and recommended supervision of the workers to make sure they conformed to strict building specifications. In the 1800s, it was common to test the strength of a wall by kicking it. The sound of loose hearting trickling down the interior was a sure indicator of a hollow centre and, therefore, loose face stones. That spelled doom for the waller!

Front Pinning

It is tempting to fill spaces between stones on the face of the wall with small wedges, or support a large stone with smaller ones (called front pinning). They are often more cosmetic than structural and highly likely to break or fall out. If a small gap must be filled, it should be done from the inside – not pressed in from the outside – so there is less chance of the wedge falling out if the wall flexes or settles. It is far better to build more tightly and not rely on small stones to fill tricky spaces.

If a small stone must be fitted in the face of the wall, it should be well secured by all those around it, and have some length to reach well back into the wall. These stones should be placed during construction, not after the event. That way there is less chance of them falling out.

Pinning was an old practice in Scotland and also noted in Bristol, England (Rainsford-Hannay, 1976). Small stones were tapped into the gaps between the face stones after the dyke was completed. This practice was also recorded in Australia, no doubt taken there by Scottish contractors in the mid-1800s. It was advocated as a way to tighten up the stones and make the wall vermin proof. This is now regarded as bad practice – pushing small stones between larger face stones is likely to force them apart. It is better to concentrate on a tight build from the beginning.

Chapter Five

Constructing a Dry Stone Wall

This section describes, primarily, the standard-pattern, free-standing, double-skinned, agricultural dry stone wall developed in the 1700s. The wall has a foundation, two outer faces of stone linked by throughstones, and is topped with a coverband and copes. Hearting stone tightens the core. It is only one of several possible ways to build a stone wall.

This accepted 'pattern' comes straight out of the descriptions of the eighteenth- and nineteenth-century writers on agricultural improvement. They enthused about a reliable, reasonably cheap stone wall that borrowed several features (foundation, throughstone, proper bonding and so on) from masonry wall construction. These writers thought dry stone walling could be done to a strict pattern and formula. The estate managers drew a straight line on the map and left it to the contractor to build a wall, to a certain specification, along that line, whatever the ground conditions.

The teams of walling contractors, working on moor and mountain, came up with imaginative ways of breaking out from the established formula to suit local conditions. They were usually paid a set amount

A dry stone wall from New Hampshire, USA, age unknown. It is low and wide, quite different from the typical British free-standing wall. There are enough similarities, however, to indicate that the building method comes from a common instinctive understanding of how to put small pieces together to create a larger, more stable structure.

An Infinitely Variable Design

This cross-section diagram of a typical 5ft (1.5m) free-standing dry stone wall is based on an A-frame similar to the one discussed earlier. The relationship between width and height is clear. This narrowing is called the batter of the wall.

The foundation stones are shown as a scarcement; they extend a few inches beyond the width of the first course of face stones. This adds to the effective width of the foundation and spreads the load of the stonework.

The part of the wall between the foundation and the coverstone is known as the double. This is divided into the first and second lift by the throughstone. The throughstone and the coverband project a little from the face of the wall.

The diagram shows the main components and sections. Any element of this pattern can be adjusted, emphasized or deleted to suit a particular stone or design need.

Each of these parts has several local or regional names. For the purposes of simplicity, this volume uses the names shown on the diagram, although these terms are not used everywhere. Wallers, whether trainee or professional, should get to know their local terminology and use it to ensure a piece of their heritage is not lost.

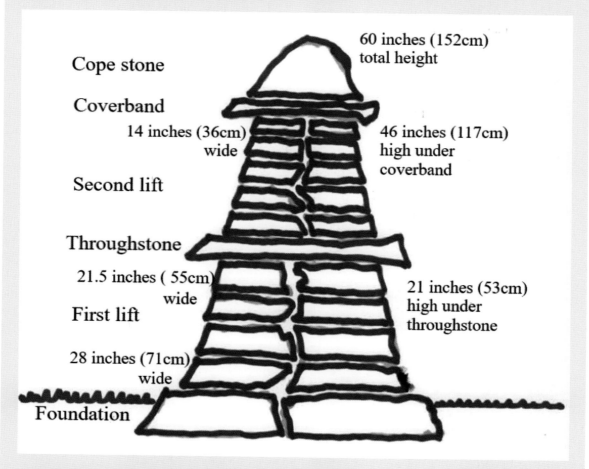

Cope stone

Coverband

14 inches (36cm) wide

Second lift

Throughstone

21.5 inches (55cm) wide

First lift

28 inches (71cm) wide

Foundation

60 inches (152cm) total height

46 inches (117cm) high under coverband

21 inches (53cm) high under throughstone

A cross-section of a typical dry stone wall. The voids inside the wall are filled with hearting. Measurements not to scale.

per yard of wall they built, and could not be held up by lack of materials or waiting for guidance from land agents. They used their initiative, and what was on the ground.

Some walls emphasize particular elements. Others miss out an element. For example, some stone walls are too wide for throughstones; some walls have no coverstones; some have a cap of flat slabs rather than vertically laid copestones.

We offer no apology for repeating this point, here and in the following pages – the appearance of the wall, and how it is built, depends on the available stone. Ground full of round boulders (for example the valleys of Cumbria, in northwest England) will produce a certain type of wall with few through-stones because there is a lack of long stones. Ground full of old shattered basalts (for example parts of the Isle of Skye) produces walls with irregular, or no, copestones because the rock shatters before it can be shaped.

The Foundation

A foundation is the interface between a structure and the ground. It must sit solidly with the mini-mum chance of slipping or being undermined. A house foundation either goes down to bedrock, is supported on a network of concrete piles, or sits on a concrete pad. Those foundations are calculated to support the weight of the structure and not move at all, or move as one solid unit.

Check Before You Dig

Before digging a new foundation, check for drains and utilities. Check surrounding buildings to see if there is evidence of services, such as downpipes or electrical cables. Many local authorities have a ser-vice confirming what's buried underground. In a rural situation, there is less chance of meeting gas, sewer or electricity services but, as the author discovered

on one site, an armoured phone cable can look like a tree root.

Think twice before building over the top of some-thing that may have to be opened up in the future, for example cables, pipes or sewers.

Creating Flexible Rigidity

A dry stone wall is flexible, made up of many pieces of stone arranged in a narrow row. It is therefore fairly vulnerable to movement. If the foundation is prop-erly laid, it takes care of seasonal fluctuations and minimizes the chance of the wall sinking, or falling to one side or the other.

Poured concrete is occasionally advocated as the base for a dry stone wall. This would be solid and stable, but expensive, especially for a rural site.

It is normally sufficient to remove the grass and a few inches of soil to form a flat, firm, shallow trench for the foundation. Don't go too deep with a foun-dation trench; there is usually no need, unless the ground is very soft or the area is prone to frost heave (*see* below).

Avoid building straight on top of grass. The grass will rot and the topsoil will crush. This loosens the stones so failure is inevitable. Dig out the trench an inch or two wider than the intended foundation to give extra room to fit in slightly longer stones, bearing in mind that no stone should venture far from the guidance of the string line.

The foundation course is usually made up of the largest stones. This has practical reasons (it means heavy stone is not lifted) and structural reasons (small stones are laid on top of big stones; big stones are not sitting insecurely on top of small stones). If there are a lot of large stones available for the foundation course, spread them out. This uses them up without breaking them, and could introduce an interesting pattern to the wall. It also provides frequent 'bookends' for added stability and strength.

The foundation stones sit directly on the ground. It is therefore easy to carve out the softer soil to conform to the shape of the stones and make sure every part of the stone has contact with the ground. Aim for zero space between stone and soil. This means more friction and less chance of slippage, and does away with the need to spend time and effort shaping an awkward boulder. The foundation is the only place in a wall where this is possible.

A foundation course might be technically perfect, but if it is laid on loose ground it will fail; a second-rate foundation built on firm ground is more likely to survive.

The way the wall is built may affect the foundation. The size and weight of the stones should be balanced from side to side to reduce the chances of any stone being forced sideways and taking the wall with it.

Proper preparation is important when laying out the foundation. When a wall collapses, it is often because the base stones have moved. Perhaps the ground became waterlogged (improper planning for drainage) or undermined (stone laid across soft ground).

A dyke built of thin Caithness flagstone. For whatever reason, the ground has sunk in the middle of the image. The stone is thin, taking many courses – around forty – to attain full height. The wall moved with the subsidence and flexed. It did not collapse or fall to one side.

This small opening was introduced into an existing wall as a drainage channel. The stonework goes well below ground level. A wet hole built up behind the wall when the immediate drainage pattern changed.

Ground Pressure

The pressure a dry stone wall exerts on the ground is remarkably small, typically around 500–600lb/sq ft, approximately 3.5–4.2lb/sq in, or 0.25–0.3kg/sq cm. A broad 'footprint' of flat stones means the weight of a wall is spread across a larger surface area. Consider the difference between a stiletto heel and a work boot. The small surface area of the heel causes damage to floor coverings. The same person's weight, spread over a boot's sole, leaves a muddy mark and causes no damage. In a foundation, one large stone, ideally a flat plate, is better than an arrangement of smaller rock because it spreads the weight and provides a stable platform for the stones above.

Scarcements

The base for a wall is often built with a scarcement. The foundation stones extend 4–5in (10–13cm) on each side, beyond the extent of the first course of face stones. This provides a wider footprint for the wall and gives it somewhere to go if stones ever slip.

A 4in-wide (10cm) scarcement is characteristic of walls in parts of Kentucky, USA. It is a way of providing a broader foundation for a wall, especially if the wall is relatively slim.

If a wall runs across a slope, a scarcement on the downhill side only provides extra support for the wall, allows for a degree of slippage and decreases the chance of undermining.

The scarcement could be a course of 6in-thick (15cm) stone for a wall crossing a pasture. In a moorland situation, a scarcement might be a levelled course of large boulders providing a platform for the wall as it crosses a slope or a dip in the ground. A scarcement also adds an attractive architectural element, which can be exaggerated for walls in a domestic setting.

In Australia, some walls were built with a significant scarcement, part of a plan to control the spread of rabbits. This, along with a deep foundation, reduced the chance of rabbits burrowing under the wall. In sheep pens, the walls often have a scarcement on the inner side of the wall to reduce the chance of the sheep undermining the wall as they run around inside. These pens also have round corners. This tends to keep the sheep moving: they cannot mob in a square corner and, through sheer force of numbers, push the wall over.

Laying out the Foundation

The string lines, set tightly from A-frame to A-frame, outline the outer edges of the foundation.

The bottom course of stones, those sitting directly on the ground, is laid tightly side by side along the string lines, with their longest edge reaching well into the centre of the wall. They can touch in the middle. Avoid one stone reaching too far across the wall and restricting what can be laid in from the other side. Short stones are not bound into the structure so well as long stones; laying the stones in equally from both sides ensures the foundation is kept balanced and provides a secure base for the upper courses.

If a short foundation stone cannot be avoided, it should be compensated for by laying a long stone above it – one that grips the short stone and ties it into the middle of the wall. Dry stone walling is a compromise. We must make do with what's available. However, the foundation is not a good place to compromise on strength.

The ideal foundation would be solid stone, all tightly laid together, with the minimum of hearting. Hearting is important but, anywhere in the wall, it is an assistant to friction and gravity, not a replacement for well-placed stone.

When laying a foundation, try to stagger the joints between stones on one side and the joints on the other side. This is the horizontal equivalent of breaking a vertical joint. It adds to the strength of a wall, allowing it to flex a little well before it breaks.

This foundation looks lopsided because some face stones (next to the yellow tape) reach more than halfway across the wall. Note how the roughly triangular stone next to it will never move once weight is on top, because its widest end is inside the wall. The foundation was fit for purpose. It was part of a low retaining wall, less than 2ft (60cm) high. The front face of the wall was well built – backed up with solidly set stone, compacted soil and compost.

A partly completed foundation for a straight section of wall. The stones are of similar height, set on a thin base of crushed rock, for drainage and to provide a solid surface. The waller has used two sets of string lines on each side to help with accurate coursing. Note how the stones are laid – long edge into but never beyond the middle. Work by John Bland.

Frost Heave

Dry stone walls are flexible. They will move with the ground if it dries out or freezes with the seasons, and this ground movement may cause individual stones to move.

In most climates frost heave is not a problem, but in parts of North America, for example, the frost goes deep into the ground, sometimes several feet. This freezes the wet soil and causes it to expand by about 8–10 per cent. The ground level rises with this expansion and forces anything on it upwards or sideways. When the ground thaws, the ground level drops down again. From discussion with a Canadian waller, it seems the problem of frost heave is more to do with the cumulative effects of several seasons of multiple freeze/thaw cycles, not one big eruption of a couple of feet in one winter. The stonework is shaken apart by many small movements rather than one big shove.

One answer to frost heave is to dig the foundation down to below the frost line, so it sits on ground that is too deep to freeze. That is obviously a lot of work, and requires a lot of building stone, or hardcore, to fill the hole. A deep trench causes another difficulty, in that it is a chance for water to gather, as it would in any trough. Even if the trench is filled with stonework, water fills the voids and may cause damage when it freezes and pushes the stone around. One way of reducing the chance of damage is to control the water. Drain it away from under the wall to reduce the chance of it freezing there. The flexibility of the wall should be able to cope with the remaining effects of the freeze and thaw cycles.

The best remedy is probably the easiest. Many walls in New England are built on a shallow trench filled with several inches of well-tamped crushed stone. This allows the water to drain away from under the wall while it is liquid, before it has a chance to freeze.

Floating Stone

In extreme situations, a dry stone wall could be 'floated' across soft, boggy ground by digging the foundation trench deeper and putting in bundles of wood. This method was used during construction of Victorian railways across the moors of northern England and the Scottish Highlands. They also used bags of waste wool. Organic material decays very slowly, if at all, in boggy ground. The bundles act as a raft to support the weight, but they must be well compacted to ensure the wall does not sink; if it does sink, simply add another course of stone.

Dry stone walls usually stop if they come up to the side of a bog, and are replaced with a post and wire fence – or not at all. The wall resumes at the other side when the ground is firm again.

Foundations are not Always Laid Flat

Foundation stones are normally laid like any other stone in the wall. The mantra is 'flat and level, long edge into the centre of the wall'.

Of course, there are exceptions. Short sections of small stones laid on edge have been recorded in foundations of walls in the north of England. These stones grip the ground better than stones laid flat, especially across rocks or soft ground.

In parts of France, the foundation stones are laid perpendicular to the batter of the wall. Face stones in retaining walls are also laid at right angles to the battered face and dip down into the middle of the wall. Upwards movement is resisted by the weight of the wall. When the movement reverses the stones should settle back down with no great damage. This is especially effective in regions where frost heave or seismic activity could force the stone upwards, or, as in the case of retaining walls, the bulk of the stonework is resisting pressures from behind.

Drainage and Obstacles

In most climates, a dry stone wall and its foundation are free-draining: water naturally finds its way

Failed Foundations

Here are two examples of failed foundations.

In the first case, the long stones on the right had been laid traced, with their length along the wall instead of into the wall. This is not a strong way to build. The weight of the wall caused the foundation stones to rotate, pushing them out and taking the wall with them. The two big stones on the left are also laid traced but they reach well into the wall and are unlikely to move. This is the best way to use them, though they took up a lot of vertical and horizontal space on one side, and were not balanced by similarly sized stones on the other side.

It was important during this repair to allow for the garden. The foundation was relaid a few inches lower to allow for cultivation right up to the stones and reduce the chance of undermining.

In order to remedy the situation, the large stones were spread out between smaller ones and dug into the ground, set leaning back to correspond to the batter of the wall. There was no harm in them extending an inch or two into the garden. The traced stones on the right were mixed with longer stones, reaching into the middle of the wall, to form a more stable foundation.

The big stones meant the foundation was fairly wide. The wall was rebuilt to about 4ft (1.2m) high, including copestones, and 16in (40cm) wide under the copestones.

In the second example, the large stones in the foundation spread apart, taking the wall with them. This was a burial ground, so it was important for the repair to maintain the aged appearance of the wall. The stones were left traced but set more securely into the ground, leaning slightly back to suit the line of the batter, and solidly hearted. Incidentally, the wall was full of gravel, a poor substitute for proper hearting. This may have contributed to the failure.

The cleared-out foundation for a collapsed garden wall, probably 25–30 years old. The red string lines, slightly askew, give the approximate line for the new wall.

The ground on the downhill side was soft and full of rabbit and mole activity. The hearting we see consists of fragments broken from the round boulders when they were originally shaped.

through. Small arches, or lintelled openings called lunkies (*see* Chapter 10), can be incorporated into a wall as a more formal drainage channel if there is an obvious need for it. These openings are also useful for taking a wall's foundations over tree roots. The wall is raised above the roots and they have room to flex and grow.

Foundations on Slopes

When building up steep slopes, the foundation course is 'stepped' into the slope like a staircase. This keeps the stones lying horizontal (instead of parallel to the ground), and gives the wall a good 'bite' into the land. A foundation on a slope is further stabilized if large stones are dug into the ground at regular intervals to act as anchors, holding back any tendency to drift. Building on dips, hollows and slopes is covered in Chapter 7.

The First Lift

The foundation course is normally laid flat, one stone thick. The stones only need to fit together from side to side. The construction of the courses on top of that are more complex, as the stones in this part of the wall have to interact with each other in every direction – above, below and to either side.

When stones meet, there is potential for strength or stress. The individual stones must be laid carefully to create a solid bonding pattern that distributes the load of the stones evenly, equalizes the pressure, and limits the chance of any stone moving in any direction – up, down or sideways.

'Movement' must not be confused with 'flexibility'. 'Movement' suggests one stone, or a group of stones, is making a unilateral decision to be somewhere else. That movement may not be reversible. 'Flexibility' suggests an in-built co-ordination where everything moves in unison, most likely from a seasonal shift in the ground – when it dries in the summer or freezes

in the winter. The wall will soon recover from this when the season changes.

Laying Stone in the First Lift

We have discussed the physics and mechanics of laying stone properly, and the importance of laying them to the string lines. Now we move on to build the first lift, the lower part of the double, between the foundation stones and the through-stones. It makes up approximately half of the height of the wall.

The largest, and the most awkward, stones should have been used in the foundation. Try to use any remaining big stones in the lower courses and mix them in with smaller ones; do not put the large stones all together while their supply lasts. Aim for some kind of symmetry in the design. If there are especially thin stones, lay them aside – they will be very useful near the top of the wall, to level off the last few inches of double, ready for the covers and copes.

Choose a stone with a good edge, one that will look decent on the face of the wall. Lay that face out to within a fraction of an inch of the string line, no further. Don't let a projecting stone push the line out. Lay the rougher end (the 'tail') of the stone into the middle of the wall. If necessary, place a smaller stone, or hearting, under the tail of the face stone to bring it into line with the batter and line of the wall.

Lay one stone, then lay another tight against that one. Don't lay one stone here, another a foot away, and a third one a couple of feet further on. That means a lot of time will be wasted hunting for exact-sized stones to fill the gaps. A dry stone wall is not a jigsaw where particular pieces have specific places. All the stones in a pile, if they are the same type of rock, will have similar angles and shapes. Learn to recognize them, and how to fit the shapes together.

Lay a stone on top of a stone; don't lay a stone then try to fit a thinner piece into the gap below it. This wastes time and is not a strong way to build.

A skilled waller picks up a good stone and makes it fit. An onlooker will express amazement at the 'right stone' being picked every time, but it's a skill that comes with practice. Just as brick and block masons lift up a standard-sized unit and immediately know what to do with it, a dry stone waller looks at a pile of stone, uses an educated eye to pick up a good one and, in the seconds between ground and wall, makes a multitude of unconscious decisions and actions to fit that stone into that gap. They repeat the process several times within a minute, with another stone. That's a super skill.

If a stone needs trimming to make it fit, a quick tap with a hammer, a wee chip off the block, is often enough. With experience you will get to know how to apply force to a particular stone type without it falling to pieces.

Take a cue from nature when laying a stone. Sedimentary rocks, in particular, have bedding planes, visible as horizontal lines of colour in the stone.

A view of A-frames and string lines, and a completed foundation with some stones laid for the next course. It shows how stones should be laid in any part of the wall. The individual stones are set tightly side by side and reach well into the middle, where some touch the stone reaching in from the other side. Each stone is in solid contact with its neighbours. The voids between the stones are filled with good, clean hearting stone, as big as the gap allows. The chance of any stone moving, in any direction, is reduced to near nil. This particular A-frame does not have a crossbar indicating the position of the throughstones; marks on the timber, at each end, will do that instead. Work by John Bland.

These are planes of potential weakness that could be taken advantage of to split the stone. Lay a stone with these stripes set horizontally; that is when it is at its strongest. Sandstones are especially vulnerable to weathering if the bedding planes are laid on edge. Water and frost get into vertically laid beds more easily than when the beds are horizontal, causing edge-laid stone to erode faster than normal.

As far as the novice is concerned, the individual stones should always be laid horizontally, level side to side and front to back, and with their longest edge into the centre of the wall. Any spaces around the stones should be solidly filled with smaller stones (hearting) as the work proceeds. If the stones are laid properly and a hair's breadth from the string line, you can't go far wrong. With experience and practice, tidy, attractive work, is inevitable.

These basic requirements make mechanical sense. A stone is at its most stable if surrounded by like-minded neighbours. It can be built on with less chance of slippage, disruption and collapse. There are occasions when, for artistic effect or necessity, a stone must be laid on a slant (from side to side or back to front), or laid contrary to established practice but, for the beginner, 'rules is rules'.

After each course of stone is fully laid, check the hearting is properly completed and raise the string line ready for the next course. If the stone is all the

Three courses of stone are complete on the nearest side of this garden wall. Note how each stone breaks the joint between the two stones below it and helps support two stones in the course above it – following the mantra of 'one over two, two over one'. The large stone in the middle of the wall is called a jumper. It 'jumps' up through three courses to provide an interesting deviation from the horizontal coursing. The stones in each course are similar in size; some were naturally that size, some were shaped. Coursing like this creates a secure flat floor for the next layer of stones. Work by John Bland.

Badly Laid Walls

The first example shown here uses good stone but has been badly laid and poorly coursed. Too many small stones fill spaces between larger face stones. Many look loose. The cope looks disjointed. This fine-grained sandstone was used for many historic houses; it is easily shaped and could have produced an attractive wall.

The stone in the second example is also of reasonable quality, but the work looks as though it has been stacked with little forethought: there has been no attempt at coursing, laying the stones level, or keeping the stones square to each other. The task has been completed as a rough jigsaw. With some shaping, the wall could have looked much tidier. There are vertical and diagonal running joints. Small stones have been used to support large face stones; most have been placed loosely, in a gap, to fill a hole. The copestones are also rough and irregular.

Rough walling.

An example of general poor building.

same thickness, raise the line by that amount to keep the coursing accurate. Otherwise, raise the lines by the average thickness of the stone.

When it comes to about halfway up the wall, the stonework must be levelled off in preparation for laying the throughstones. In the A-frame we saw earlier, this point was indicated by a crossbar. The throughstones will lie right across the wall, and it is important to have as flat a bed as possible for these important stones.

Some walls do not have throughstones because long stones are not available. Even so, it is still a good idea to bring the wall to a level at the halfway point, to set up a good, stable base for the upper stonework.

Options for a Half-Completed Wall

When the wall is levelled off, ready for placing the throughstones, it is the ideal height for a 'sitting wall' or a platform for a table or flowerpots. The top of such a platform is best secured with flat stones or flagstones. Make sure the top slabs are reasonably thick: a 2in (5cm)-thick slab on top of the wall looks flimsy, while 4in (10cm) looks more substantial, provides an attractive edge, and reinforces the idea of stability.

The Throughstones

The throughstone, also known as a through, thruff, binder, tie stone or through band, is a strengthening feature, incorporated into the wall, usually halfway up the double.

Throughstones lie all the way across the wall. They link the outer faces, tying them together. They provide strength and a rip-stop, a strong point to limit the extent of a collapse. They also act, like any face stone, to break the joint between the stones in the course they are sitting on. This means they are providing a strengthening link up and down, as well as across, the wall.

The throughstone is ideally one long stone. If long enough stones are not available, two stones, one from each side, interlinking in the middle, are a good substitute. The throughstones are comparatively large: they may be several inches high and, in some rock types, over 12in (30cm) wide. Careful packing and pinning are essential to ensure they are in solid contact with everything beneath them. If they should ever move it will upset the stones around them and weaken the structure. Do not leave any voids.

Nowadays, generally speaking, throughstones are placed at 1-yard or 1-metre centres (36in or 1m between the centre of each stone), halfway up the face of the wall. This allows for some being wider than others and keeps them equally spaced. Placing of throughstones varies from region to region. If in doubt, have a walk around nearby walls and adopt that pattern.

The course of face stones between the throughstones must be carefully laid, perhaps more carefully than elsewhere, because the throughstones take up so much of the space. Hearting continues to be vitally important.

Tourists, and others 'not in the know', often think projecting throughstones are steps. They are not. Local practice determines whether the throughstones stick out from the face of the wall. They may project on one or both faces of the wall, or be flush with both faces. When throughstones protrude on only one side, this has been interpreted as an indication of ownership.

In the nineteenth century, projecting throughstones were evidence the landowner demanded, and the wallers produced, to confirm the wall was constructed to a specified design. Proof of throughstones gave the land agent one less reason for withholding payment. Throughstones took time to produce and lay. The wallers might be tempted to go for quantity rather than quality at a time when they were paid by the yard of completed work.

In certain circumstances, throughstones should not protrude; for example, cattle could use them as a rubbing post and destabilize the wall (though they

A collapsed section of dry stone dyke. The unravelling has been stopped by the throughstone (about halfway up the wall) and the coverband (the flat stone at the top of the double, under the copestone). Both these long stones perform a similar function: they reach entirely across the dyke and help bind it together.

Throughstones are set. In this particular wall they project a few inches beyond both faces. Note the four lines on each side of the wall; the waller used these lines to keep the coursing level and, as each stone was placed, help the decision-making process. Work by John Bland.

This wall has two sets of throughstones. Both sets extend a little beyond the face of the wall. Note how the course of stones above the throughstone bridge the joint between the throughstone and the face stones built up each side. This would be an easy place to allow a running joint. Part of this wall is ready for the copestones. Note how the stones are coursed with the larger stones at the bottom (where there is the most room). Thinner stones sit near the top. This image also shows the extent of hearting between the face stones. The wall is, as near as possible, solid stone. Work by John Bland.

can be deterred by a strand of barbed wire, a yard from the face of the wall). Throughstones should not project in sheep pens or anywhere where they might interfere with smooth movement.

Two, even three, sets of throughstones have been recorded in particular dry stone walls. One set is placed part way up the wall and the other sets are placed at equal distances between there and the copestones. Each throughstone in an upper course is placed midway between two in the lower set. Extra throughstones provide more strength, especially if the building stone is small.

Some early writers (from the comfort of their drawing rooms) recommended carrying throughstones to the site if none were found locally. That could be hard work if the source was some miles away so, unsurprisingly, the wallers preferred to use what was immediately available.

Some local stone types, for example the limestone areas of southern England, do not have a lot of long or large stones. Wallers in those areas use the longest available stones as some sort of throughstone. These are laid in from each side and may interlink in the middle. The lack of long throughstones is compensated for by a tighter build, something which is more easily achieved with soft limestone.

In parts of Scotland and Canada, throughstones made from cedar wood have been recorded (Rainsford-Hannay, 1976). This is an interesting instance of vernacular construction – an easy fix to a local situation.

In a garden setting, throughstones may be exaggerated or multiplied to provide shelves or planting opportunities.

The throughstone course is levelled off before the string lines are raised for the start of the second lift.

The Second Lift

The second lift is the body of wall between the throughstones and the coverstones and cope.

The build procedure is the same as for the first lift. The wall narrows towards the top of the wall, as we see from the shape of the A-frame. The face stones usually become smaller and thinner. The heavy stones have been used in the lower part of the wall. This is lighter work, and faster.

For the topmost part of the second lift, it is especially important to be guided by the line. Lay stone out to the line, and up to the line – and no further. This makes sure the top is as flat as possible. With practice this is easily achieved, even with rough stone. Properly laid stones guarantee a secure support for the coverband and, therefore, the copes above, as well as ensuring a smooth front face to the wall, with no bulges.

The top courses of face stones must never be laid traced. There is no way to compensate for a traced stone in the top course, unless the coverstone or copestone is expected to perform that duty. Each stone's longest edge must lie into the middle of the wall to ensure the weight of the coverstones, and the copestones is spread evenly over the top of the wall, not concentrated on badly laid stones sitting on the edge.

The wall's width at the top of the double should be no less than 12in (30cm), preferably nearer 14 or 15in (35 or 38cm). This provides a wide, secure base for the coverband. If the top is too narrow, it cannot provide a stable base for the weight of the top stones. If the top is too wide, there may not be stones long enough for a conventional coverband or cope.

A view along the top course of a limestone wall, showing the face stones extending into the middle of the wall. Hearting fills the voids. The wall has been brought to a level – something which initially looked impossible for such rough stone. More hearting is required before setting on the coverband and then the copestones. This wall is fairly wide with a slight batter. Inis Oirr, Ireland.

The Coverband

At the top of the second lift, the coverband, the collective name for the coverstones (also known as covers), performs a similar function to the throughstones. They are long stones laid across the width of the wall as a continuously connected course on top of the double (the body of the wall between foundation and coverstones). The coverband ties the top of the horizontal stonework together and provides a solid base for the copestones. It also supports and distributes the weight of the copestones evenly above the double.

The copes sit more securely on the relatively flat surface of a coverband than resting directly on top of the double.

Coverstones must be placed carefully, tight against each other. The procedure is not complicated. Set one coverstone. Make sure space under it is filled with hearting stone and pinned solidly, to ensure it sits on the double. This increases friction and inhibits movement. After attending to the needs of one coverstone, lay another hard against it, trimming it if necessary to ensure a tight side-to-side fit. Pack under that, then repeat until the section is covered.

A course of coverstones has been laid across the top of this wall, ready for the copestones. The local limestone provides plenty of flat stones, long enough to lie across the top. Inis Oirr, Ireland.

The covers often project a few inches over each side of the double. In old agricultural walls, this projection acted as an additional obstacle to deter livestock, particularly sheep, but even rabbits, from jumping over. In domestic or feature walls, longer coverbands make an attractive overhang or shelf.

Coverbands are not found in every wall. The copestones are often laid directly on top of the double. Long stones, if they are in short supply, are better used as throughstones.

In regional walling styles such as the Galloway dyke and feidín wall (*see* Chapter 6), the coverband is about halfway up the final height of the wall, and supports most of the weight of the stonework. These were highly effective 'sheep walls', built to enclose sheep pastures in the eighteenth and nineteenth centuries, when big profits were made from wool.

Copestones

These topstones are also known as cams, toppers or capes.

The top of a wall is the first thing to catch the eye. The copestones, along with the coverband, tie the top of the wall together to protect it from weather and disturbance. The cope also acts as an additional element to 'terrify' livestock and thwart their attempts to jump over. Old accounts of walling frequently tell us that a precarious-looking cope will deter even the most determined sheep.

The cope was, and is, a chance for individual expression. Bear in mind the need to conform to, or at least consider, the local style when repairing or adding to an old wall, or building a new wall near an old one.

The top section of a wall could be as simple as a peaked pile of small stones, sometimes called a rubble or puddle cap, straight on top of the double, or on top of the coverband. It could also be flat stones set vertically on edge, flat stones canted at an angle, slabs laid flat across the top or trimmed boulders sitting directly on the double.

The norm for a cope in Britain is flat stones set vertically on edge, and that is the style described in the rest of this section.

A nearly completed dry stone wall in a domestic setting. The coursing is immaculate. The thickness of the stones in each layer decreases with height, up to the perfectly flat top line under the copestones. String lines were used to indicate the height of each course. The stones were carefully selected and shaped to fit within the designated height of the course. Note also how the course of stones above the throughstones carefully covers what could be a running joint if it continued beyond the side of the throughstone. Work by John Bland.

Agricultural walls usually have a cope at least 10 or 12in (25–30cm) high, as it needs to look in proportion to the rest of the wall and have some sort of 'presence'. One course of 12in-high (30cm) vertical stones saves the time and effort of building three or four courses of horizontal stones.

The height of the copestones is set by stretching a string line across the top of two vertical copestones of the required height, one at each end of a stretch. Copestones are shaped and laid on top of the covers or double, so that they stretch across the width of the wall. The top of the cope should just graze the string line. Any short copestone is brought up to the required height with a small flat stone or shim under it. Use one shim rather than two or three stones jammed into the same space – it looks tidier.

Cope a wall in longer sections, perhaps after two or three days' work on the body of the wall. This smooths out the line of the cope and avoids it looking like a series of short stop/start events.

If good copestones are in short supply, make do with what is on site. Set the best ones at intervals and fill in between with smaller stone or carefully placed broken stone, using a string line to keep the top level. Close up, this may look disjointed, but from 3 yards it will look fine. Looking from 10 yards away, the top line of the wall will appear neat and tidy. The aim is to go for a smooth line, avoiding any jagged outcrops.

Any cope looks better with a couple of inches overlap on each side of the double. This ensures a more efficient grip on the stones below, and, incidentally, creates an attractive shadow line.

Medieval walls around monastery pastures in northern England had copestones overhanging on one side, reputedly to keep wolves out of the sheep pastures (Lord, 2004). In Australia, there are examples of overhanging copestones, sometimes with added timber slats or wire netting, to prevent rabbits from jumping over.

The wallers of previous generations would have restricted their copestones to what was immediately available. Nowadays, we can choose a contrasting stone for the cope, based on texture and colour. This, of course, comes at the cost of time, material and budget.

The Locked Top

This type of cope was reputedly developed in south-west Scotland in the 1750s. The vertical stones are laid tightly against each other and tightened further with stone wedges.

A vertical cope on a dyke in the Scottish Highlands. The body of the dyke needs some attention but the cope is a fair example of flat slabs, some cut from boulders, placed vertically on top of the stonework without a coverband. These copes take some effort to push off. The cross incised into the stone in the middle of the image is said to mark the centre of Scotland.

An example of a vertical 'locked top' cope, without a coverband. This dyke, in the Scottish Hebrides, was built with stone recycled from ruined croft houses.

The body of the wall, between the cope and the throughstone, has suffered damage; the top stones remain vigilant. The cope consists of two courses of rough boulders, tightly fitted together. The tight-set cope is behaving like an arch, buttressed by stonework on each side of the gap. It will survive like this until something else moves. This damage is best repaired by taking down the suspended copes, rebuilding the face stones and resetting the copestones. Without attention, the dyke will eventually fail and allow sheep to escape. Galtee Mountains, Ireland.

Elegant Copes and Country Cousins

If the rock is easily shaped, and the extra work can be justified, more refined varieties of coping are possible. These copes take more time and effort to produce and are therefore less likely to be seen in field walls.

There are many ways of topping off a wall. The aim is to provide a secure top and be reasonably decorative without being overly expensive. The only limits are the available material and the imagination of the waller.

A more refined cope with occasional taller stones, made from an easily shaped sandstone. This wall surrounds a Scottish estate. Helmsdale, Scotland.

Carefully cut half-rounds, set on top of a thin coverband, top off this wall between a house and the public road. Caithness, Scotland.

Another variation of cope from Caithness. These triangular copestones sit on top of a low wall separating a street from the riverside walkway.

A Caithness cope using rougher stone, with very little shaping. This is a field wall. The cope does not need to be so refined as wall tops around a house or farmyard.

A sandstone cope, often described as a 'cock and hen' cope in reference to the up-and-down nature of the alternating small and large stones, often even more regularly spaced than this example. This decorative variety of coping mixes up the stone and avoids having a length of good copes followed by a length of rougher pieces. The jagged nature of the top was originally thought to act as an effective deterrent to livestock. Tayside, Scotland.

An interesting and imaginative arrangement for a mortared cope, from West Cork, Ireland. Vertical pieces of the local shale are separated by round fieldstone. The lime mortar has weathered with the stones. This cope differed from others in the immediate area. Perhaps it indicated a boundary of some significance. Perhaps it was an individual expression by the waller, or maybe there was not enough suitable shale for the cope. This 'mixed media' cope would have been faster to build than a cope consisting of half-inch-thick sheets of shale.

A view along the top of a wall in Kentucky, USA. The copestones present a uniform vertical face when viewed from the side. They meet in the middle of the wall. The interior is then jammed with smaller stones, in the manner of a locked top. This centre lane is often filled with mortar to deter stone thieves.

This limestone wall is topped off with a slightly domed arrangement of stones bedded in mortar. It looks reasonably attractive once the mortar has weathered. Inis Oirr, Ireland.

A cope on a relatively wide wall in Langdale, northern England. The water-tumbled stones are not long enough to span the top of the wall. The top courses of stones are chosen from the largest available and slightly canted back towards the middle of the wall. The core is filled with smaller stones. Over time, they are joined by stragglers and material picked from the fields. In a domestic setting, this wall top could easily accept a covering of turf.

New England capstones. Vertical copestones are not common in New England. They are often openly resisted and, if seen at all, are usually the result of British influence. These capstones lie across the wall like a course of coverstones. The walls often have little, or no, batter. Rhode Island, USA.

Coping on a Slope

Coping a wall on a slope should be started from the downhill end. The process for building a vertical cope is as described below.

First, set a large stone on top of the wall to act as a solid stop, to resist the pressure of the copestones leaning down on it. Set another cope at the right height some distance up the wall.

Stretch a string line between the tops of the two stones, making sure it is at a constant height above the wall over the length. Select and lay copestones to sit tight on the top of the double or coverstone, to within a hair's breadth of the line. Work uphill, placing each stone vertically or leaning downhill, according to the local style.

Just like coping on the level, lay longer sections at a time, rather than sections of just 5 or 6ft (1.5–2m). This gives the cope a smoother appearance over the length.

Remember, gravity is our friend. Each copestone is pushing onto the one downhill from it. There is maximum stone to stone contact, and this will get tighter with time. After a section of cope is completed, tighten it even more by tapping flat stone wedges between the individual copestones to make a good locked top.

Sometimes copestones are laid canted, or leaning to one side on a slope. In parts of Kentucky and Yorkshire, for example, copestones traditionally lean downhill. These are not large stones, but usually thin, flat pieces. Laying them this way means they are sitting more tightly together than when placed upright. There is more friction between the individual stones and they can only get tighter. Care is required to ensure the angle of lean is consistent. Laying the copes still starts from the downhill end.

Laying a cope so that the stones lean uphill on a slope means the waller must start from the top – play with bricks or biscuits to see why. This option requires extra care to ensure the individual copes sit firmly on their base and won't slip downhill while the copestones are laid, or loosen with time. If a larger copestone is placed every few yards this will help strengthen the cope.

Planting on Top

Thick sods of grass and soil (not the thin slices of turf meant for lawns) are a viable topping for a dry stone wall, especially in areas with high rainfall.

Use two layers of sod. The first layer is set with the grass side down onto the stones, and the second layer sits on top of that, with the grass side up. This gives the best opportunity for sustained growth – there is a thick layer of earth below the top grass. A top-dressing of earth will hold the turf in place until it establishes itself. This topping should quickly grow into a healthy sward, with the roots helping to bind the stonework together. Plants with more vigorous roots are not recommended, as they would eventually disrupt the stones.

The top of a wall can be converted to a kind of flowerpot for more sophisticated planting. This works particularly well on a wide wall. Leave out the hearting in the top 6in (15cm) and carefully align the top face stones for maximum space between. A daubing of clay would make the cavity more water retentive. The top of a wall is similar to a rocky crag: it is dry, hot and free-draining. Fill the cavity with good water-retaining compost, enough for succulents or drought-tolerant plants. Wall tops incorporating any types of vegetation may need irrigation to survive the summer.

A Canadian wall topped off with a type of sedum. This hardy plant has survived several freezing winters and dry summers without any irrigation. This spiral, part of a longer wall, was designed and built by Eric Landman and his team.

Adding Height to a Wall

Sometimes an existing wall must be made higher, if, for example, the land use changes from arable to grazing. Sheep jump higher, and more often, than turnips. The height of some walls could be increased by removing the coverstones and copestones, adding a few courses of stone, and replacing the top stones. Another option would be to add a course of long stones to lie across the existing cope.

This is impractical if stone has to be carted some distance, or is not available.

The height of this dry stone dyke was raised with posts and two strands of barbed wire on each side. Livestock respect this barrier and the landscape still benefits from the shelter and aesthetic value of a well-built dry stone dyke. Incidentally, if cattle are likely to use a stone wall as a rubbing post, a single barbed wire strand, posted a yard from the wall, will keep the beasts at bay. Farmers have also been known to put a tall stone in the field for cattle to rub on, and had that mistaken for an ancient monument. Southwest Scotland.

The higher copestone, cut from sandstone and bored for two wires, adds height to the wall and keeps it from looking too 'agricultural'. This feature must have been incorporated as part of the original design. Variations of this style use regularly spaced upright stones or timber, some with notches, to support wires or poles.

The effective height of this wall is increased with iron posts, fixed into the stone. The posts were inserted into drilled holes and secured with molten lead, or lead punched in around the iron post with a pointed chisel. Another option was molten sulphur. The hole need only be a few inches deep.

Coursing

The terms 'course' or 'coursing' have been used in other sections as general terms for a tier, a run or a layer of stones, along a wall. This section discusses the term in the sense of whether the walls are 'coursed' – laid in distinct layers; 'random' – where the layers are less distinct (sometimes non-existent); or 'random brought to courses' – where irregular stone is used in various size combinations to create distinct horizontal layers at several points over the height of the wall.

In mortared stonework, overlong horizontal lines are shunned, being regarded as an indication of a line of weakness. Is this also the case for dry stone work? We shall leave the question unanswered.

Generally speaking, flat or symmetrical stones look awkward when they are not laid level. If the stones are all about the same size, the walling tends to be coursed – that's the best way to put the pieces together. Wallers using rough irregular stone produce a more jumbled pattern. There will be a mix of larger stones, reaching up through two or three courses, with thinner stones by their side. This can be a very attractive, especially if the waller tries for some symmetry in the pattern.

Nowadays, walling tends to stress the importance of working to courses, or random stonework brought to courses. Arguably, the skills required to work with misshapen, broken stone are being overlooked as agricultural walling gets less publicity, and more walls are built with flat stone in gardens and public areas. It is a definite case of horses for courses. Coursed stonework looks better in a domestic or urban setting than a wall made of rough stone.

Let's simplify things and consider the differences between coursed, random and random brought to courses. Whatever term we apply to the different ways of laying stone, they have evolved as the best way to get maximum strength with least effort for particular types of stone.

Coursed Walling

In coursed walling, each layer is made up of stones of the same height, so there are distinct horizontal lines along the face of the wall. The top edge of any particular course is flat and level, making it easy to lay stones on top. In its purest form, the stone is all the same size, from the bottom to the top of the wall. It may look a little like brickwork.

Good coursing with Vermont fieldstone. The courses lie truly horizontal even though the wall is built up a slope. Each course is made up of stones the same thickness, or combinations of stones to make up that thickness. In more refined coursing, all the stones in the face of the wall would be the same, or would be thicker in the bottom courses, becoming increasingly thin in the upper courses. We should also note the vertical copestones, the stepped foundation and the projecting throughstones – the square-ended granite pieces. Work by Jared Flynn.

A more common variation has the stone in distinct layers, all the same size in one layer. The courses of stone decrease in thickness towards the top of the wall.

Some types of stone are easily coursed, for example Caithness flagstone, Cotswold limestone and some Yorkshire sandstones. Aberdeenshire granite was cut into uniform sizes for use in coursed dry stone dykes. Some dykes in Royal Deeside, Aberdeenshire, have coursed cut granite on the roadside face and more randomly laid stone on the field side. Coursing is difficult or impossible, however, with some stone, especially if it does not come in regular sizes or takes too much time to shape.

Accurately set lines, and working to them, is essential for good coursing. This keeps the individual stones level and square, and produces a nice, even appearance. There are no wavy lines on the face of the wall. Stones must be laid level; if one stone is not laid level, it is difficult to build on top of, and the one on top of that is even more difficult to build onto.

A coursed dyke from Caithness, Scotland. The stones in each layer are all about the same thickness. Occasionally combinations of two thin stones make up the height required. Coursing is easier when the local stone comes in thin beds with straight edges.

Another coursed farm dyke using the local Caithness stone. Note the inclusion of taller stones called jumpers. They 'jump' up to provide a link between the different layers of stone and, arguably, make a stronger wall. They also make the face of the wall more interesting – not something the agricultural waller thinks of, but worthy of consideration if the dyke is in a domestic setting. These jumpers are bigger stones and must be laid carefully, especially if they are sitting on top of smaller stones. Lay them as normal, on a solid base, never traced and never, ever on edge. If the jumpers had been equally spread in the face of the wall, it would be even more attractive.

Random Walling

In random work there is no intention to arrange the stones in strict layers, all the same size or height. There are not many continuous horizontal lines along the face of a random wall.

Random style is often forced on the waller because the local geology consists of rock types with no consistency in shape or size, for example shattered sandstones or weathered basalt; the waller has to work with what's there.

Random work can be as tight as coursed work, although it will have more irregular bonding patterns, as must be expected with odd shapes and sizes fitted together. This type of build has been described as 'random rubble', reflecting the irregular stone and how it is put together.

Working with these rough stones takes practice. It is more like the jigsaw puzzle to which dry stone walling is often compared, and tends to confound those more accustomed to using predictable limestones or flat-bedded sandstones.

String lines are set as normal for random work. There is no expectation that one particular course will be brought to a level, apart from throughstone height (if the wall has throughstones) and the top of the double. The lines guide the batter and straightness of the wall, and are raised from time to time, once they have been reached or passed by the majority of stones on one layer.

A dry stone dyke built to a random pattern. Note the substantial throughstones and the covers and copes. The dyke was built from broken boulders and local schist. There is no real attempt at levelling off the stonework, apart from at throughstone level and under the coverstones. Building lines were used to indicate batter and straightness, rather than coursing. Strathmashie, Scotland.

Random Brought to Courses

In this variation, the irregular stone is levelled off, using combinations of thick and thin, at several points in the height of the wall. This creates a distinct flat surface – visible as obvious horizontal lines along the face of the wall – and re-establishes a baseline for the work on top. This is similar to the levelling-off for throughstones, or the flat top of the double before setting the coverstones or copestones.

This variation is ideal for tall walls built out of rough stone.

A transition from random to coursed. Round river-washed stones and the local slate combine to bring the stones to a level and accommodate the larger wall end stones. Additional strength is needed at that point. Cumbria, England.

This wall is built out of irregular stone. It makes best use of large stones, avoiding the unnecessary work of breaking it up. Large stones and flatter ones are combined to form distinct layers of stone and a flat top line. This presents a pleasing pattern to the eye and makes for a stronger wall. Cumbria, England.

This wall is not coursed in the accepted interpretation of the term, but there are indications the waller worked to a line and laid similarly sized stones together, especially in the top half. Larger stones are mixed throughout the wall. The term 'organized' seems more appropriate than 'random' or 'random brought to courses'. Roscommon, Ireland.

Disruption in the Ranks

This good, flat stone could have been laid better — more evenly coursed from bottom to top. The large jumper in the middle raises concern. It is laid on edge, as indicated by its bedding planes, breaks up what bonding pattern there was, and probably lies two-thirds of the way across the wall. This leaves less room for strong bonding on the other side. Awkward gaps are filled by small pieces of stone, which are likely to fall out. The large stone is best broken up and reused as smaller, coursed pieces.

A mix of poorly laid stone. The large stone gives quick height but disrupts the coursing.

Chapter Six

A Gallery of Wall Types and Bonding Patterns

Different Stone, Same Principles

By now the reader should know that there is an established method and pattern for double-faced dry stone walls. There is also a great variety of them – just like there is a basic recipe for scones and hundreds of interpretations – because the local ingredients are different and the skills of the baker, or waller, vary from place to place.

It is relatively easy to work with straight-edged flat stones, but walling advice for such material appears vague and inappropriate for places where stones are shaped like French bread rolls with a twist in the middle, or square lumps with sharp edges. Most stones are irregular. Some boulders are like flat ovals. Some rocks break into misshapen cubes or thin sheets.

Early descriptions of walling from the 1700s and 1800s tended to assume flat rock was the norm, and included illustrations with perfectly interlinked stone. These specifications were adopted by the land agents, who passed them on to wallers working with the realities of broken sandstone, shattered granites and basalts with no definite shape. The wallers learned to be flexible. They adapted the basic design to suit the local stone and had enough work in their locality to develop and finesse a particular style of wall.

A standard pattern for single walls is less obvious. Closer inspection shows us that the principles of breaking the joint and placing the length of the stone across the width of the wall (rather than into the middle, as with a double wall) are a common feature. This applies whether the stones are round boulders or flat slabs. If these basic principles were not applied, the wall would simply be a pile of stones.

Some walls do not, at first sight, appear to follow the 'normal' principles of 'proper' dry stone construction, such as breaking the joint. On closer investigation, they do, however. The objective is always to create the maximum friction between the surfaces, whether the stones are laid horizontally, vertically or diagonally.

Some kind of wall is possible with most types of stone, providing it has a bit of length to it.

A wall made from concrete core samples. The corner is mortared concrete blocks – a 'bookend' to hold the round shapes in place. Cores naturally fall into the most efficient pattern, like honeycomb. Note that, even when the stones fit tightly together, there is still a lot of unoccupied airspace, reckoned to be over 20 per cent, in a well-built wall. This sounds high but that figure does include all the space within the wall and between the face stones. Seattle, USA.

A double dyke, over 150 years old, and a close-fitting construction in the real world of irregular stone. The flat faces were made by splitting boulders with a sledgehammer. Spalls, a by-product of the splitting, fill in between the larger stones. Badenoch, Scotland.

A roadside retaining wall in Mallorca, Spain. Each piece of the relatively soft limestone has been shaped. Stones fit tightly together, with no shims or pinnings between them. The builders worked to produce maximum stone-on-stone contact. The vertical column of square stones strengthens the structure and 'bookends' the smaller stones.

This massive dry stone retaining wall illustrates a bonding pattern more usually associated with mortared masonry. Note how two thin stones fit beside one thick stone and how the joint between any two stones is broken by the length of the stone above. These stones were carefully laid by machine. The top edges were cut back with hammer and chisel to correspond with the batter of the wall. The image also shows the perfect interlacing of the corner stones. Kentucky, USA.

A tight bonding pattern on a smaller-scale dry stone wall, using rougher stone. This careful interlinking produces a strong bond with maximum contact between individual stones. This bonding pattern is ideal for flat stones, especially for this easily shaped Kentucky limestone.

Mellow Yellow

In this example, the builder used his skill to mix thick and thin stone to produce good coursing. The larger stones in the centre of the image overlap the joint between the two directly below. We see where thinner stones are laid on top of each other to equal the height of one thick stone and offer a secure base for the course above. One thick stone on top of that covers the joints. This is good building practice when the thickness of the material varies, creating maximum contact between all the stones, vertically and horizontally. Movement of the stone, from side to side or up and down, is nearly impossible.

There are gaps where stones do not sit tight beside each other. We should not be too critical; this wall dates back to the 1800s and is still functioning well. Most likely the gaps arise because the waller did not trim the stone too much. That would have taken time and was not cost-effective for an agricultural wall. Over a square foot of area, these small spaces could be regarded as faults; over a 200-yard wall the irregularities become a pattern, part of the charm of dry stone walls.

An old wall of thin-bedded Caithness flagstone in the north of Scotland. Yellow lichens and moss have taken advantage of the rough surface. This stone splits down into thin pieces and is relatively easy to work with – although, being so thin, it takes many courses to make the full height of a wall.

A dyke built from a hard sandstone in southern Scotland. The stones are tightly fitted together, despite the irregular shapes. This rock type breaks to reasonably consistent angles that are easily rearranged so they fit together. The local dyker recognizes this and can work quickly with such stones. Wallers from the Cotswolds, on the other hand, who are used to working with smaller flat limestones, might struggle with this rock for a few days until they get used to it.

This wall seems disorganized, compared to others we have seen. The stone is rough granite, in many shapes and sizes. Despite that, the dykers have produced a substantial double dyke with a nice top line. Large boulders have been incorporated into the foundation, perhaps moved only a few feet from where a glacier dropped them. Small, tightly fitted stones stabilize the larger ones. This is definitely not a wall with delicate coursing but it is strong, performs its function well and is, in its own way, good-looking. Badbae, Scotland.

An old sheep pen in Badenoch, Scotland. The bottom courses are made up of large stones. Some stones have fallen out and the wall looks remarkably hollow; there seems to be a lack of proper hearting. This has not weakened the wall as the large stones are well laid. The top half of the wall is more finely detailed – an alliance of flat stones and split boulders produce a tighter fit.

This double-skinned agricultural wall is intriguing. Try to imagine the sequence of construction. Horizontal stones and vertical stones sit together. Joints are broken horizontally and vertically. Smaller stones are laid in whatever way contributes to the height of the wall. One question (which resolves itself after some thought) – is that horizontal stone in the middle a lintel? This fractured limestone lends itself to this apparently chaotic build. A wall built out of flat-bedded sandstone or split boulders looks entirely different. Inis Oirr, Ireland.

A Celebration of Irish Limestone

Sean Scully, described as an 'abstract expression-ist artist' (2019), found inspiration and compari-son between his artwork, bold blocks of colour and the stone walls of western Ireland. He describes the walls of Aran: 'These walls are silent. And yet this sculpture is like the music of this place: austere and elemental.'

At first sight, these walls appear to have little in common with those in Scotland and England, but closer examination reveals they were built with a full understanding of the benefits of friction, gravity, symmetry and balance.

This wall, from the Irish Aran Islands, is built from limestone, some prised from the limestone pavement. Friction between the stones keeps them upright and strong. The wallers placed tall upright stones at regular intervals to stabilize the structure horizontally and vertically, and reduce the chance of collapse. The stones are laid with maximum contact between each other, often with their longest edges totally across the width of the wall. The surface of individual stones is fairly rough, which contributes to the friction.

A single wall from western Ireland. At first sight, the stone looks unorganized. Stones are laid any way, very few horizontal, and there is no coursing. If we look carefully, however, we see there is a considerable amount of stone-on-stone contact. Groups of small stones are buttressed by larger stones. Each stone is well supported by those around it. There is, literally, nowhere for them to go. This is a strong wall, well able to stand up to Atlantic storms. The open nature of the stonework allows the wind to filter through. If the wall were a solid barrier, with no gaps, a storm would be more likely to blow it over.

This is almost an art piece, made out of limestone slabs. It might be called a 'lace wall' in New England because of its open tracery appearance. These walls have attracted the attention of artists, who see them as a series of attractive spaces held together by a web of stone. The central feature is a vertical section of flat slabs buttressed by stones leaning in from each side. Other vertically laid sections buttress diagonally laid pieces. If we look carefully, we can imagine the sequence of construction. Despite the open pattern, there is a lot of stone-on-stone contact and joints between stones are broken. The Burren, Ireland.

An Irish single wall built of rough boulders. The weight of each stone lies solidly on those below. They are jammed together, spreading the load to form a solid structure. It is definitely not rabbit proof, or even small child proof, but it does hold back sheep and cattle. Tall versions of this type are still built in the Mourne area of County Down, Ireland, using a JCB to do the heavy lifting. Not that long ago, human muscle did the same work, assisted by planks and prise bars.

This limestone wall, in County Roscommon, Ireland, features rounded stone. It contrasts with the flat pieces of limestone found further west in The Burren. These double walls look very like those from parts of Scotland, another sheep-breeding area.

A square corner in a limestone wall. The interlinking of the stones at the corner is similar to other, tighter work. The stonework leading to the corner is a fascinating tangle of verticals and diagonals. This work may look casually thrown together but in reality it is well organized. Inis Oirr, Ireland.

Getting down to the Skeleton

How the stone is laid is just as important as how much stone is laid.

The Bailey Island Bridge in Maine is 1,150ft (350m) long. It was completed in 1928 and refurbished in 2009/2010. It is built from 10,000 tons of granite billets, each approximately 8ft × 2ft × 2ft (2.4m × 0.6m × 0.6m). They criss-cross each other, laid so that the joints between two stones are broken by the stone above. The bridge carries a two-lane roadway. That tonnage of stone, over that distance, for a structure that wide, means the stonework is very thin, and the bridge is practically see-through. The majority of the volume is empty space, held together by elegant stonework.

Gravity and friction, as always, play an important part in the bridge's strength and stability. The process has been refined as far as it can go. Is it too much of a stretch to compare this bridge to the carefully planned strengths of a rose window in a Gothic cathedral?

The road could have been laid on top of a long causeway made up of a solid pile of granite. That would be strong but would use far more granite, need more maintenance, and take up more ground than a bridge. A solid barrier would also cause difficulties with the local tides. Creating something slim, strong and stylish was worth the extra effort.

The cribstone method of construction meant most of the stone processing was done at the quarry. This reduced the cost of transporting uncut stone to the bridge site, as well as the cost of moving waste. A large part of the total cost was pushed to the material side of the equation. In everyday walling, the cost of material is relatively cheap, as the stone is often delivered to site as rough, unprocessed rock. The costs are biased towards labour and time on site.

The Bailey Island Bridge in Harpswell, Maine. Note how the granite pieces interlink, breaking the joint between the stones below.

Exaggerated Copes

We usually think of the cope of a wall as a single course of stones set on top. In two outstanding examples (the Scottish Galloway dyke and the Irish feidín wall), the copestones have become a significant, even dominant part of the wall. These walls are a combination of single and double walling. The double makes up the lower section and the single is the upper part. This type of construction achieves height with minimum effort, and uses the local stone to best advantage. If large plates of rock or boulders are on site, it is sensible to use them as they come, without going to the extra effort of smashing them up and working with a pile of small pieces.

The Galloway Dyke

In southwest Scotland there is a local style of dry stone dyke that is now recognized as 'the Galloway dyke', although when this pattern of was first developed, it was simply described as 'the sheep dyke'. Many hundreds of miles of these dykes were built to enclose sheep pastures.

The dyke is brought to approximately half height by normal double construction. A set of continuous coverbands is then set on top, about where the throughstones would be. This course is a secure base for the upper half of the dyke, a substantial section of single – in effect an exaggerated cope.

This design spread, with regional differences, depending on what stone was available. It is particularly common in areas of wild moorland or mountain where the local geology consists of rough sandstone, basalts or granites. The dykers relied on stone from the immediate area as there was no access to finely quarried stone. They used what was on or in the ground, or what could be pulled from a nearby crag.

The tight build at the foot of the dyke helped make it rabbit proof. This was certainly seen as an attractive feature when Scottish and Irish wallers were contracted to Australia in the late 1800s to build stone walls on sheep stations.

A-Frames and lines can be used to keep the lower section of a Galloway dyke straight and level. After the coverband is set on, the lines are of little use, however, as the stones are too irregular – apart from a top line to set the final height.

It takes considerable effort to construct the top half of a Galloway dyke or feidín wall – it is a two- or three-man job. This dyke was surely built with co-operative effort. The heaviest stones were lifted 4 or 5ft (1.2–1.5m). There are practical difficulties to lifting these large stones without disturbing the smaller stones on which they sit. The task is easier if they are slid up a plank, scaffolding poles or even a ladder. Nowadays, a tractor's hydraulic power performs this service. Northwest Scotland.

A Galloway dyke using round boulders. The exaggerated cope overhangs each side by several inches and was originally deemed especially effective in containing livestock. The spaces between the round boulders are filled with smaller stones and angular spalls broken from the larger boulders. Southwest Scotland.

Shattered stone is used for a variation of the Galloway dyke. The angular nature of the pieces means a tighter fit. Despite the irregular material, the dykers managed to bring the top course to a remarkably flat line. Southwest Scotland.

The Feidín Wall

The feidín wall is acknowledged to be a version of the Scottish Galloway dyke, most likely taken to Ireland from southwest Scotland by landlords working to improve their Irish estates in the 1800s. The design was adapted to suit the local stone. Excellent versions of the feidín wall are found in western Ireland, in east Galway, the limestone Burren and the Aran Islands.

There are two variations of the feidín wall, described in McAfee (2011). One, from east Galway, is very like the Galloway dyke from Scotland. The bottom half is a double-faced wall consisting of two 'skins' of stones, with hearting in the middle. A course of flat stones (in effect a coverband) is laid on top of that. A carefully arranged cope, made up of flat vertical pieces, laid across the width of the wall, makes up the total height.

In another variation, from further west in The Burren and the Aran Islands, tall, wide, slabs are set into the ground at regular intervals. One long edge of the slab lies across the width of the wall to stabilize the smaller stones on each side; these stones are known as 'mother stones'.

A double-faced wall is built between the uprights, to about half the total height of the wall; these small stones are described as 'children stones'. This section of the wall normally has little or no batter. A continuous course of flat stones, similar to a coverband, is then laid across the top.

A vertical course of stones is laid on top of the flat coverband. These are the copestones, sitting one stone wide, all the way across the top of the wall. If individual stones do not make it up to the intended height of the wall, smaller stones are set on top. These have become known as 'father stones'.

This spectacular cope secures the stones in the lower half and, like the Scottish locked top, adds height quickly and easily without the effort of putting together several horizontal courses. It also avoids the need to break up large slabs.

This section of wall, complete with a lunky, is very similar to a Scottish Galloway dyke. Galtee Mountains, Ireland.

A frame and lines are used as normal, to keep the bottom half of the wall (the double) straight, or nicely curved, if that's what the design calls for. As with the Galloway dyke, the frame and lines are far less useful when setting the upper sections of the wall, unless the intention is to achieve a very refined look. In that case, lines are used as normal to define the upper and outer edges of the stonework.

The limestone karst landscape of western Ireland provides a sufficient mix of small stones (collected from the fields) and slabs (prised off the ground) to create this unique-looking wall, an example of the western Irish feidín wall. It is clearly comparable to the Scottish Galloway dyke.

A taller version of the feidín wall, still recognizable as a development from the principle and appearance of the Galloway dyke. Inis Oirr, Ireland.

Consumption Walls

Some dry stone walls are obviously significantly wider than others. They may be a wider by a foot or so, some are a few yards across. These are called 'consumption walls' and were built wider from the time of original construction. The name derives from their function of 'consuming' the stone from the land they sit on.

Consumption walls are a way of using up large amounts of stone. When land was cleared, drained, ploughed and limed, something had to be done with the stone. Carting it away was not always a viable option. Building a wide wall was an easier way to put stone out of the way of the plough and the mower.

The best, most organized, of these have two good faces of stone (laid like in any double wall) and a very wide interior filled with stone.

A wide wall, built to clear the pasture of stone. The wall is wide enough to include small alcoves for sheep shelters. County Wicklow, Ireland.

A consumption dyke, top view. This wall has two well-built outer walls up to five feet high. The centre of the dyke becomes a safe plateau for wildlife and plants. Note the recently added stones. Torphins, Scotland.

The width of these walls means they cannot have a formal cope. The top stones on each side are laid tight, often slightly tilting down towards the middle of the wall.

The famous Kingswells Consumption Dyke in Aberdeenshire, Scotland, is massive. One part of it is 33ft (10m) wide at the top, 7ft (2m) high and 1,440ft (440m) long (HES, 2008). A quick calculation, based on the stone weighing 2.5 tonnes per cubic metre, gives a weight of well over 20,000 tonnes. This consumption wall is an exception – most are a lot smaller. It dates from the mid-1850s and was part of a larger land improvement scheme.

Building a consumption wall follows the same techniques as for a slim field wall. Obviously, there is little or no chance of finding throughstones or copestones for a wall this wide. It starts as a foundation course; then the sides are brought up as normal. Rough stone and small stone fill out the middle. If there are any long stones they should be spread out, reaching into the wall and adding to the strength of the outer faces. The batter for a consumption wall would be the same as for the narrower double wall.

It seems clear that construction of this type of wall starts out with the final size fully planned in advance. Presumably a judgement was made about the amount of stone available and a calculation decided the dimensions of a wall big enough to consume that amount of stone.

There is less need for new consumption walls nowadays, as most land that needs to be cleared has been cleared. The way these massive structures were built can be adapted, however, to create a raised platform, a massive retaining wall or a recreation of ancient burial cairns.

The Clava Cairns, a series of Bronze Age chambered cairns in the Scottish Highlands, are very similar to consumption walls, though built for an entirely different purpose, and nearly 4,000 years before the consumption walls we know. The common feature is the accumulation of a large mass of stone in one structure. Large kerb stones contain a mass of smaller stones to form a solid mound. More details are available in the links noted in the list of specialist topics at the end of this book.

Consumption walls are easily repaired. Consider them as an extra-wide double wall with some characterstics of a retaining wall, due to their width. These walls need a solid face to contain the mass behind.

Stone-Faced Earth Banks

The stone-faced earth bank was an early combination of stone and earth. Over time it developed into several interesting local variations, including ones that incorporated a hedge in the side of the wall that faced into the field. The growing hedge disrupted the stones but was a solid barrier to livestock.

This design flourished and is still common on the west coast of England, where the climate is usually wetter; this keeps the vegetation on top of the wall alive. Many of these wide structures are topped off with a hedge or turf.

The stones are not large. They are laid vertically with their longest edge into the earth or subsoil core. That core is compacted against the stone face as the build proceeds. One variation is the Welsh *clawdd*; others are known as Cornish hedges, Devon banks or Cumberland banks. They share common features though the design varies from district to district.

Welsh *clawdd* are typically 3ft (1m) high and 3ft (1m) wide at the top with a batter of one in six. For a more detailed description of this type of wall, *see* the reading list for specialized topics at the end of this book.

Gabions

Gabion baskets are not really dry stone walling but deserve a mention because they are often advocated as a cheaper option, especially as retaining walls on

A stone-faced earth bank based on the Welsh *clawdd* wall, built as a low retaining wall. Carefully placed stones protect an earth core. The outer face consists of stones laid vertically, tight against each other. Note how they are set in horizontal rows. Each stone sits over the join between the two below it. Compacted earth or subsoil fills the space behind the stones and holds them in place. In this particular example, a shallow batter adds to the strength of the wall; the face of the wall is not steep.

The remains of a Scottish variation of the stone and earth bank. Note the dip in the ground in front of the stones. This may have been a ditch to add to the wall's effective height. Trees have grown through the stonework and the top stones of the wall have toppled over. These fences might have worked for cattle, but are less useful for sheep. Inverness-shire, Scotland.

embankments, riversides and domestic situations. They are a viable option if correctly installed.

The term comes from the Italian *gabbione*, meaning cage. Gabion baskets are a wire cage packed full of stone. They cannot be relied on to bear weight unless they are backed up with a steel or concrete frame to support the load.

These baskets are typically filled with appearance, colour and texture in mind, rather than strength. If the intention is to replicate the general look of a stone wall, the metal cages should be carefully filled using

the standard dry stone building principles of proper bonding and hearting. It is important to make sure there are no empty spaces in the middle; once weight is put on top of a badly packed gabion basket, it will quickly distort.

The Dominus Winery in Napa, California is an excellent example of an architect-designed building that uses the principle of the gabion basket to produce an attractive outer skin. A steel superstructure carries the main loads. The open stonework is a good way of regulating the temperature of the building.

These gabions have been badly filled, especially the top one. The stones are laid on edge to make the package look good, but add nothing to strength. There is every chance the wire cages will buckle and the structure collapse.

Chapter Seven

Special Circumstances and Obstacles

How to Start and Finish a Wall

The body of a dry stone wall is typically built of horizontally laid stones, carefully placed and held together by friction and gravity. The end of a wall requires something rigid to hold it tight, something vertical, to stop the horizontal stones from unravelling.

The simplest wall end is a large stone or a flat slab set into the ground. Failing that, arrangements of large stones, solidly set, will suffice.

The most common way of forming a wall end, or wall head (called a 'cheek end' in Scotland), is to lay headers (long stones reaching across the wall) and stretchers (long stones reaching along the wall) in alternate courses up to the required height. This is topped off with a large stone to act as a large 'bookend' to support the copestones. The profile of the wall end is the same as the wall – as taken from an A-frame.

The A-frame is best set some inches from the proposed end of the wall, to allow access while building.

A gateway in Caithness. The stonework leading up to the gateway is carefully built. The vertical slab provides a solid end for the wall and protects the horizontal coursing. The slab has been shaped to match the profile of the wall and is drilled to take gate hinges.

A vertical slab used for a gateway in a post-and-wire fence. This is equally applicable to gateways through stone walls or hedges. Cherish such stones – they are useful and difficult to replace.

A large block of basalt buttresses the end of a wall made from 3in-thick (7.5cm) andesite.

This finely detailed work displays all the aspects of a good wall end. The headers reach across the width of the wall and the stretchers lie along the wall. Note how they interlink at the face to create strength. The sixth stone from the bottom is simultaneously a header and a stretcher – one long, wide stone covering the work below. Also note the excellent curvature of the wall, the coursing and the large end stone to secure the cope. Work by Daniel Arabella.

A typical wall end on an Irish sheep farm. It uses the local stone, with the minimum of shaping. The stones on the face of the wall end are laid tightly together to maximize the forces of friction and gravity. A pair of these, at each side of a 10ft- or 12ft-wide (3–3.5m) gap, with posts a few inches inside the gap, would create a cattle-proof gateway. Fixing hinges to a stone in a wall end is not recommended, as there is not enough strength in a normal wall end to resist the leverage of a swinging gate.

Large boulders, set carefully on top of each other, make up a solid cheek end. These walls are one stone wide – single walling. This one was most likely built in 1853. One post remains of the pair that originally supported a gate. The dyke's function has been passed on to a post and wire fence. Glenisla, Scotland.

String lines are used as normal. The face of the wall end should be vertical or very, very slightly leaning back. A wall end is often associated with a vertical gatepost. If they are both vertical, the gateway will look co-ordinated.

It is preferable to build a wall up to a fixed gatepost rather than finish the wall end and then dig a hole immediately in front of it for the gatepost. That could disturb or undermine the stonework.

A wall end can be built as part of the first work on a new site. If there are no obvious stones for the wall end, consider starting to build a few yards from the end, wait until sufficient suitable stones are found, and then build the wall end.

If there is good stone on site, start right away with the wall ends. Lay out the foundation for the wall end at the same time as the rest of the wall. Work from one end of the section towards the middle, then build the foundation for the other wall end and work from there towards the middle. This keeps the ends strong. Any weakness now lies well away from the ends.

Wall Ends Gone Wrong

A wall end's position and responsibilities make it exposed and vulnerable, so it is especially important that a wall end is built on solid ground. Digging out the soft ground and replacing it with a solid base of hardcore, and adding a subsoil scarcement, would help spread the load.

It is always a (minor) quandary whether to put a header or a pair of stretchers as the foundation stones for a wall end. The choice comes down to the available stones and how to best use them.

A good broad footprint is essential in soft ground. The small stones in the foundation here sank into sandy soil. The large stones in the upper tiers followed until they were stopped from total collapse by the gatepost. Using the longer stones for the foundation, instead of up in the wall, would have resulted in a stronger build.

This wall end has some causes for concern. There are some good stretchers but no good headers. This creates a running joint up the face of the wall end. The stone in the foreground corner (second from the grass) is laid on edge. One point supports the weight above. The thin stone to the left of the block (fifth from the bottom) is laid traced and on edge. A small point supports the stretcher above it. The weight of the wall comes down onto two small points. Compare and contrast this with earlier images of wall ends.

Walls on Curves, Circles and Arcs

Curves

Building a gently curved wall, a tight curve, a semicircle or a circle is not much more difficult than a straight section. Stones are placed the same way; hearting is just as important. The placing of throughstones, coverstones and copestones is very similar. If the curve is very tight the stone may have to be shaped to fit. At an extreme, the individual stones might need to be shaped like slices of a pie or pizza to make them fit securely together. Happily, most curves are gentle and stones are fairly irregular. They can accommodate all but the tightest curves with a minimum of shaping.

The strength of the stonework, as always, depends on maximum horizontal and vertical contact. Make sure stones are solidly gripped and cannot slip out. Joints should be thoroughly broken, with weight sitting solidly on each stone, and a maximum of side-to-side contact. Build tight with the minimum need for hearting. These small stones are essential to tighten the face stones, but there comes a point when too much hearting can reduce the amount of friction between stones.

Extra care and attention are required to keep the batter of the wall, and the line of the curve, consistent.

Building a curved retaining wall is simpler than a free-standing wall on a curve, as the retaining wall only has one face that needs to look pretty. Everywhere behind the front face stones can be jammed solid with the rock infill and hearting; strength here is more important than appearance.

In a free-standing wall, the concave curve on one side of the wall is mirrored by a convex curve on the other side. Lay stone carefully. Set throughstones accurately, and make sure there is a good link from face to face. Check dimensions constantly to make sure the wall does not become pinched or narrow over the length of the curve.

A curved section could be built freehand but, in order to ensure consistency of the dimensions, some sort of guidance and planning would help.

A spirit level attached to an angled piece of board is one way of keeping the batter accurate. Laying a garden hose on the ground is recommended as a way of drawing out a gentle curve.

A-frames set along a curve can provide the same guidance as they do for straight walls. Try to keep the number of frames to a minimum, otherwise the stonework becomes entangled in a web of guide lines. Two frames, one at each end (where they can be consulted for dimensions), and lengths of rebar, set at the angle of the batter along the length of the curve, are often sufficient. Line stretched from rebar to rebar gives the height but, of course, does not outline the curve. The curve has to be judged by eye and kept 'sweet' by frequently checking the batter and the width of the wall, using the dimensions taken from the A-frames or a plan.

Circles and Arcs

A firepit is the smallest usable round structure. This could be as simple as one course of stones arranged in a circle, shaped so they fit tightly together. This small number of stones can be laid freestyle, by eye. Pick stone that won't be affected by the heat of the fire, with maybe a central ring of steel or old truck wheel to keep the fire off the stone.

Laying out the perimeter for a round-walled enclosure requires slightly more effort. Large-scale full circles can be drawn with a string line pivoting from a set point, usually a pin hammered into the ground. From that point stretch a string, representing the radius of the circle (half of the diameter) and travel all the way round, with some kind of marker, to draw out the circle. That circle could be the inner or outer face of the wall. Decide what the width of the foundation is, then lengthen or shorten the line by that amount and pivot around the set point again, marking as you go. You will now have two concentric circles. The space between the two circles is the width of the foundation of the wall.

A semicircle or arc is drawn using the same method, just going round part of the perimeter.

After establishing the centre point and the extent of the circle, semicircle or arc, it is not difficult to set up a vertical post and a trammel. The trammel can be as simple as a length of wire or a string line, with some sort of marks on it to indicate the inner and outer edges of the stonework. The vertical post must be at least as high as the final height of the wall.

The stones for any particular course are laid according to the distances indicated by the trammel. Some might need shaping to conform to the curve, but they should fit as tightly as possible, side to side. There will be an inner and an outer set of face stones, with hearting and throughbands, just as there would be for a straight section of wall.

The batter of the wall is taken care of by drawing a plan to indicate what the distance of the inside and outside face of the wall is, from the central pin, for a particular height. The plan could be a design on paper, or an A-frame built to show the profile of the wall. The trammel is raised after each course is completed and a spirit level is used to confirm it is set horizontal. At that point, refer to the plan, put new marks on the trammel and lay the inner and outer stones to the corresponding distances from the centre point.

This process is equally useful for a bench, round sheep pen or a small tower. The vital thing is to establish a datum point from which all measurements are taken, to conform to the measured plan. Refer to that plan constantly. Attention to detail is essential to get the shape right.

These semicircles were drawn by setting a vertical piece of rebar and stretching out a string line to scribe the inner and outer edges of the foundation. The batter was judged by eye – quite easy for such a low wall.

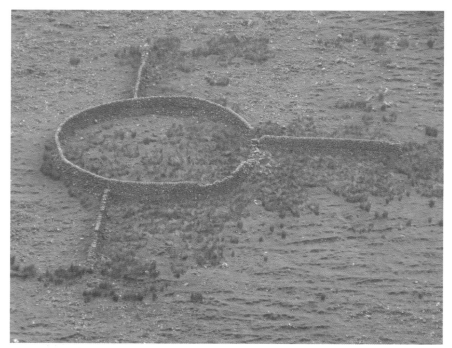

An old stell from the Galtee Mountains, Ireland, built on exposed ground as a storm refuge for sheep. There is only one entrance, on the sheltered side of the circle beside the right-hand 'leg'. The wallers must have decided on a centre point and used a string to draw the perimeter. The position and accuracy of the legs were also decided by string lines.

This semicircular sitting area, of discreetly mortared stonework, incorporates a flagstone bench and a curved back, both using cut flagstone. Various layers of stonework were co-ordinated from a central datum point – a metal pin set vertically in the ground.

A rear view of the semicircular seating area – tall slabs laid against a block core, all guided by a string line from the datum point.

This tower is about 200 years old, the remains of a windmill that pumped water from a quarry. It is a fine example of a dry stone building with a tight curve and a batter. The courses of stone must have been planned carefully, and cut before coming to site. The tower had to be high enough for a wooden superstructure with sails. The construction emphasizes breaking the bond and getting the maximum surface-to-surface contact – especially important when the body of the windmill had to resist all kinds of forces, including the torque of the sails. The doorway is an outstanding example of flagstone cutting. This stonework has its roots in ancient construction methods and is built to a far higher standard than most dry stone walls. Castlehill, Caithness.

Brochs

The ultimate in round dry stone structures in Scotland is undoubtedly the broch, which dates back around 2,000 years. More than 400 of these ancient roundhouses, mostly in ruinous state, sit in prominent positions around the western and northern coast of Scotland. There are equivalents throughout Mediterranean Europe, in particular the *nuraghi* of Sardinia, which predate the brochs by hundreds of years.

This is walling on a much grander scale but built using the same basic principles.

The ruins of Dun Telve broch in Glenelg are impressive (HES, 2020): an external diameter of 60ft (18.3m), internal diameter of 32ft (9.8m) and a height of 34ft (10.2m). The original height may have been nearer 44ft (13.3m), judging by a similar broch at Mousa in Shetland. A passageway within the walls allows ascent up through a stairway. The precise nature of any roof or internal flooring plan is still being researched.

Details of the exact method of construction are not totally understood, but it may have involved something as basic as a vertical central pole with a trammel, a plan showing the relationship between height and width, and a specialized work crew who moved from site to site.

Access details for more information on brochs and plans to recreate one are given in the specialized reading list at the end of this book.

These ruins give some idea of the work involved in building a broch, the ultimate round dry stone structure. Some of the stone is showing stress cracks – not unexpected after 2,000 years. This cross-section of the outer wall exposes the passageway between the thick stone walls. Glenelg, Scotland.

The remains of a broch. The straight edges of the severed walls indicate the ruin has been stabilized in the recent past. Glenelg, Scotland.

Corners

Consider a circular field and a rectangular field, both with the same area. Both have walls for the perimeter but the length of wall round the circular field is shorter. This might suggest there are some advantages to circular fields. In practical terms, however, an arrangement of circles on the landscape does not make sense because of the wasted space between adjoining circles. Rectangular fields are a more efficient use of land, and fences, and fencing material.

Dry stone walls round those fields frequently change direction. This could be via a gentle sweeping curve. More likely, reflecting their use as property boundaries, the change of direction is sudden, and best expressed by a square or curved corner.

Square Corners

Constructing a right-angled corner with stone requires good material, very like that needed for a wall end. Ideally, the waller can choose from a collection of long, flat stones. Some may need shaping to ensure maximum surface-on-surface contact. It's no use if a long stone arches over the stones under it, or only makes contact at two or three points; if those points crush down, the corner will loosen and fail. The pressures and weight of the corner must be equally distributed and transferred back into the body of the wall. If the weight is badly loaded onto the point of the corner, or to one side, it is likely to fail.

A corner could be built as the first part of a new wall. In that case, set up two sets of A-frames and lines (four frames in all) at the point of the corner. The lines will cross at right angles and give an accurate outline of the corner, so it is clear exactly how to lay the stones to conform to straight edges and good batter.

An alternative is to build the two straight sections of wall and leave a gap for the corner until you have some experience with the stone and have found suitable stones in the pile, or brought them to site. Make sure the straight sections will intersect as a right angle.

Stones set on the outside face of a square corner, alternating header and stretcher. The header for one leg of the wall becomes the stretcher for the other leg. Stones reach across other stones for maximum strength. The construction sequence is a variation on that required for wall ends. The corner is not two wall ends meeting at right angles: it is one unit with interlinking stones. Kentucky, USA.

Building a Square Corner

The top figure is an idealized representation of one course of stone at a square corner. Stone B, like the stone in a wall end, stretches along the wall, ending up with a face on two edges of the corner. Stone A lies across the line where the two 'legs' of the corner intersect. The duty of the other stones in the corner is as for any face stone: they should sit tightly together, break the joint and so on.

The bottom figure shows how the direction of the long stones changes on the next course. Stone D lies along the wall until it has a face on two edges. Stone C lies across the end of stone A and into the middle of the wall.

On the third course, the build returns to the original configuration of stones, as per the top figure.

Maximum surface contact between courses is essential. Chip, chisel or grind the stones to create the maximum amount of friction between them. The corner should be, as near as possible, solid stone.

Extra throughstones in the length leading up to the corner will also add more strength.

The diagrams show the stones fitting tightly against each other in the centre of the wall. In practice, the stones are unlikely to be as tight as this, at least not until the upper courses of the corner. Hearting or pinning will fill up the voids. This should be done carefully – ideally one space filled with one stone. Gatherings of small stones are inclined to crush together, which creates space and thus the possibility of movement.

Extra care is required to ensure joints are broken, especially if all the long stones are about the same length. Take your time; do not cut corners.

This sequence of stonework also provides a strong link between two walls if, for example, they meet at a T-junction, or when they cross each other.

If the corner is not an exact 90 degrees, the same principles of interlinking still apply, although some stones may need shaping to fit the angle.

If there are not enough suitable stones for a right-angled corner, consider a curved corner.

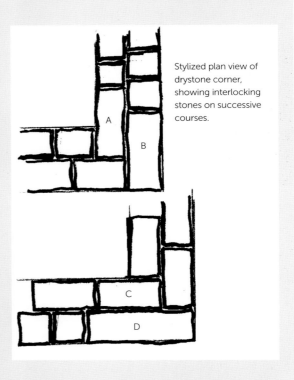

Stylized plan view of drystone corner, showing interlocking stones on successive courses.

A simpler way of setting lines is to use the frames for the outer lines and set a length of rebar or timber for the inside of the corner – set at the appropriate angle to indicate the two angles of batter going into the corner, one from each straight section of wall.

Curved Corners

A round corner can be accomplished by building the two straight sections (using frames as normal) to within, say, 6 or 7ft (about 2m) of the corner's turn, then building by eye to connect the two sections. Pay special attention to batter and straightness by frequently comparing the dimensions to those in the already completed sections of wall.

Some arrangement of lines and frames could guide the build, but access over frames and strings can get unwieldy. A single line, stretched over the stonework between two vertical pins and back from the point of the corner, is usually enough to establish height and help keep the coursing reasonably consistent.

Whatever the profile of the corner, make sure the foundation is secure. A solid scarcement under the corner would add strength.

A curved corner in a sheep fank, Sutherland, Scotland. This is easier to build than a squared corner. A curve does not need so many of the long stones associated with wall ends or square corners. The curve's batter is constant on both sides of the wall, even though it was most likely built by eye. Some stones have been shaped to form the curve. The fallen stone must have loosened when the wall settled; the corner sits on wet ground, as indicated by the vegetation.

Rounded stone, showing how it can be laid to achieve a tight curve, or a corner. Choosing the stones carefully often means very little shaping is required. A throughstone in the wall provides additional strength.

Building on Dips, Hollows and Slopes

Dips and Hollows

A long wall almost certainly crosses dips and hollows, whether it traverses a moor or a garden. If there are long, slow inclines (up or down), the wall follows the ground; but when it comes to a sudden and sharp depression, like a gully or a ditch, some extra work is needed.

The inconveniences of gradient in an apple orchard are insignificant when compared to the challenges faced by eighteenth-century wallers. They worked to a plan that, often as not, showed the route of the wall as a straight line across a moor or up a hillside. It was up to the skill of the wallers to overcome whatever obstacles were along that line.

On a slight slope, or gently undulating ground, a wall proceeds as though it were on flat ground. The A-frames lead the way along the chosen route, measuring the daily rate.

The bottom string line, as set for the foundation, will indicate if the ground dips between the A-frames. Where there is a slight dip in the ground, the wall usually flows straight over. Depending on the extent of the dip, an extra course or two of stone may be necessary to fill the space and bring stonework up to the same height as the rest of the foundation. The construction then proceeds as normal.

The shape of an A-frame tells us the width of a dry stone wall decreases with height and increases with depth. If the depression is substantial, and the angle of batter is continued, the width of the foundation could be twice the size before it reaches the bottom. That would involve a lot of work. Simpler, and more attractive, options include building a section of single walling or a wide, vertical, section of double walling to take the stonework up to a height from where the 'normal' foundation takes over.

A boundary dyke crossing a moorland landscape. From a distance it looks like a flowing ribbon of constant height. The relationship between the copes and the throughstones is constant. In some places the dyke is built with a more substantial foundation, or extra height in the upper part, to compensate for a dip in the ground. In effect, the placement of the cope and throughstones is measured from the top of the dyke. Badenoch, Scotland.

The foundation for this dyke was dug deeper to overcome a wet hole. The dykers used their skill to take the dyke over that and up the slope, while maintaining a fairly smooth top line for the copestones. The individual stones are, in the main, laid horizontally and do not slope with the ground. Badenoch, Scotland.

Steep Slopes

A stone laid directly on a sloping surface wants to slide, and furthermore encourage those around it to follow. If the slope gets steeper, up to the point where a walker would benefit from steps, the wallers do just that – the foundation course is 'stepped' like a staircase. The foundation stones are laid in these stepped cuts, sitting horizontally and secure. The stones in the upper courses are also laid horizontally.

Building on a slope starts at the bottom and works uphill. The stones will tend to bind more tightly together as the weight bears down from the upside. If the building work started at the top, the stones would tend to loosen as they inevitably slip downhill. The waller always aims to take full advantage of his constant companions – friction and gravity.

One way of adding extra strength to a section of wall on a slope is to build a wall end every few yards.

This creates a solid 'stop' and will absorb the downward pressure from the uphill section and reduce the chance of the wall buckling to either side. Another, less sophisticated, way of tying the wall to the ground is to dig large boulders into the ground at intervals. This method is especially helpful in mountains or moorland where, by chance of geology, large, rough stones are usually in plentiful supply.

Setting A-frames and string lines for a slope can be awkward. The most straightforward way, especially for rough stone, is to set the frames vertically, at the top and the bottom and build the stones between, taking care to lay them horizontally, 'stepping' into the slope where necessary. The lines will be parallel to the ground's slope. They are an indication of direction and height, not of coursing. The individual face stones will be at an angle to the string line because they are laid horizontally, not parallel to the ground.

A limestone dyke climbs a steep slope, ascending like a staircase. Foundation stones are laid horizontally in steps dug into the slope. This ensures all the stones sit solidly and that subsequent courses will not slide off each other. Durness, Scotland.

A Californian wall climbing up a slope. The stone is good and flat and easily handled. The foundation on this wall was stepped. Work started from the bottom of the slope. After a few courses, and vertical gain, longer lengths of horizontal walling were established and construction proceeded as normal.

A free-standing double wall on a slope. Note the horizontal coursing. Building started from the bottom of the hill with a solid wall end or cheek end. The coverband, under the copestones, mirrors the stepped foundation. The foundation was laid with a scarcement extending a few inches on each side, beyond the face stones. This extends the footprint of the foundation and provides extra stability. Excellent work by Stuart Joynt, Kentucky, USA.

This old wall is made of slate, boulders and quartz-rich rock. Combinations of round and flat stone keep courses level and tidy. The wall is brought to an even top line that matches the slope. The top runs parallel to the general gradient and averages out any irregularities in the ground. Construction started at the bottom of the slope and moved uphill, which kept the stonework tight – the stones pressed against their downside neighbours as the work proceeded. Ballachulish, Scotland.

This dyke clambers up the slope. The line of the existing dyke dictated this route, and the dykers took full advantage of the static rock and the footholds it provided. Note the horizontal coursing. Glenisla, Scotland.

In places where the slope is steep and suitable stone was available, dykers often altered the build from double to single. This dyke is sitting on the shoulder of a large boulder that lay in its path, obviously too big to move. This section was built uphill, from the right-hand side to the left-hand side of the image. Glenisla, Scotland.

Sometimes the slope is too steep. Here a cheek end terminates the dyke at the edge of the crag. The dyke butts into the bottom. The gap was secured with a metal post-and-wire fence. Badenoch, Scotland.

In the accompanying images of walls built on slopes, we can see that strict coursing on a steep slope means the upper course at the bottom of the slope could become the lowest course a few yards further up. Care should be taken to ensure copestones and through-stones are at a consistent height above the ground.

Walling off the Level

Despite all the 'rules' described above about laying stone, it is often a good idea not to lay a stone flat and level. Note, however, that the length of the stone still goes into the structure. Laying a stone on edge, with a short reach into the wall, is little more than tiling, and will require some sort of mechanical or adhesive support.

Walling on the Edge

Vertical copestones are the most obvious occasion when stones are set on edge, and are a good example of a vertical strengthening feature on top of horizontally laid stone.

In areas where the stone is soft, for example Cotswold limestones, the stone is tilted towards the outer edge to deflect rainwater. This helps keep the centre of the wall dry and reduces the chance of weathering and frost damage. In the Scottish Borders, some dry stone dykers also tilted stones towards the outer edge, and this practice was adopted by the local landowners for building mortared house walls to help keep the interiors dry.

Any stone sitting on edge wants to fall to one side: that's simply gravity in action. This leverage hastens structural failure unless the stones around it compensate or support it. In normally laid horizontal stonework, the ends are buttressed by vertical stones or a strongly built wall end. Most instances of vertical stonework are accompanied by solid buttressing of some kind, at one or both ends. This could be a section of tightly built horizontal walling, a pillar or a large boulder.

Setting short stones on edge, tight together, is a good way of providing a stable foundation course across soft ground or rocky ground. It is more stable than two or three flat stones set horizontally on top of each other. When the weight of the wall bears down onto the edge-set stones, they bite into the soft ground or the rock, and, unless the ground is really soft or steep, they will stabilize and not shift any further. This technique is found in southeast France for foundations crossing rocky ground, or to allow water through. It is also recorded in the north

of England for crossing soft ground. If the stones sink into the ground a few inches, it is no great effort to add some stones to reclaim the height.

Laying stones on edge is also an option when reinforcing a riverbank. If the water current undermines the stones, they will tend to sink into the riverbed rather than be washed out. It is still important to have a long edge reaching well into the bank, and that long edge must be strengthened and supported by other long edges, properly backfilled with well-placed hearting.

This technique was used on a larger scale in civil engineering; many harbour walls have stone laid on edge. This technique produces a strong wall that resists the sea crashing against the face. When a wave hits, the air pressure is allowed to escape up the vertical spaces between the stone. Flat-laid stones are more likely to be forced up, blowing the wall apart.

Thin sandstones, limestones, shales and slates lend themselves to being laid vertically. This produces a stronger build than when they are laid horizontally. One important point – the stones have a long edge sitting vertically and, for maximum strength, they must also have a long edge going into the centre of the wall.

The 'one-over-two' principle has been reinterpreted as 'one-beside-two' for this section of harbour wall. Contrast the vertically laid stone with the horizontally laid buttressing to the right-hand side. Crail, Scotland.

Edge or wedge walling, whether vertical or slanting, is a style of walling particular to areas with thin stones, such as shales or the like. This example, from West Cork, in Ireland, is built from local sandstone and shale. The overhanging copestones are made from larger pieces of the same material.

The exposed interior of a damaged wedge wall. Note how the stonework is vertical on both sides, and stones from each side meet in the middle. This requires careful placing of smaller stone in the centre to keep the face stones square on and secure. West Cork, Ireland.

An example of edge-placed stone from Kentucky, using the local limestone in what locals call a 'diagonal fence'. These fences consist of wide stones reaching all the way across the wall and smaller stones going part way from each side – in effect the same principles as used for a 'normal' horizontally laid double wall. The image includes a section of horizontal walling as a buttress, and a diagonal fence with thicker stone on the left. The canted stones fit tightly together. Each stone tooths into the joint between the two in the course below. Note how each long, tall face stone has two to the side of it, in an adaption of the 'one over two; two over one' principle. The style may have been imported by Irish immigrants.

Occasional stones should reach all the way across the width of the wall – the equivalent of through-stones in a horizontally laid wall. These are usually flush with each side of the wall.

This is another example of a type of stone wall that makes best use of the local geology. It makes no sense to break long, thin stones up into small pieces when they can easily be put on edge to form a wall.

A wall with stones laid vertically, or near vertically, is very similar to a wall of horizontally laid stones: think of it as a wall build on its side. The stones must still overlap. There should be no running joints – they would appear as horizontal lines, not the vertical lines we see in a wall of horizontally laid stone.

The build sequence is straightforward. A pillar, or section of horizontal walling, is constructed to act as a buttress. A course of vertical stones is laid on edge, tight together. This is the foundation. These stone are laid alternately high and low so they can accommodate the bottom edge of the stones in the next course. Each course of thin stone bites into the gap between the two vertical stones below it.

The stonework is laid up to the chosen height, using shorter and shorter pieces until it comes to a level top line. In some styles, for example in West Cork in Ireland, thicker, vertical copestones are laid on top, with an attractive overhang. The weight of the vertical copestones presses on the lower stones, keeping them tight. The strength of the cope is enhanced by tapping thinner shims between the individual copestones, just like the Scottish locked top.

Herringbone

In a herringbone pattern, courses of stones are set diagonally in alternate directions to create a chevron shape.

Slabs and Pillars

Some stone types naturally break into slabs, posts or pillars. Kansas limestone and Welsh slate have been formed into fence posts and used like their wood equivalent – several yards apart, with wire stretched between.

This fusion of criss-cross and herringbone patterns is an attractive – and strong – way to build a retaining wall out of small stone. The ground level at the back comes up to the copestones. Note how the joints are broken in every direction. The stones sit comfortably together, and none are overstressed. It would be more difficult to make a strong free-standing wall with this pattern. Edinburgh Airport roundabout, Scotland. Built by David F. Wilson, designed by David F. Wilson and Keith Horner of Turner Jeffries landscape consultants.

A flagstone fence from Caithness, Scotland. Some beds in the local flagstone quarries split into thin sheets, which are easily shaped. These individual flags are only a few inches thick. When they are dug into the ground and set tight, side to side, with a long edge along the line of the wall, they make a good, secure fence. This particular example has been backed up with a hedge and fronted by post and wire to keep livestock off the stone. This is truly where we could find a stone wall 'a mile long, a yard high and an inch thick'.

A 'Scotch fence' from County Carlow, Ireland. These cut granite pillars sit tightly together in a row to form a secure fence. Typically, they are 3ft (1m) high with stones 11in (28cm) thick. Part of the total length of the stone is dug into the ground. It must be tempting to acquire these hard-won stones for lintels!

This wall, made from vertical slabs of mica schist, replaced an old wooden rail fence. Slabs are set across the line of the wall, each separated by a small block of stone near the top. Built by John Shaw-Rimmington and Shawn Kelly, with input from Paul Lindhorn. Point Arena, California.

The Carlow fence, a unique combination of pillars and lintels from County Carlow, Ireland. This is an arrangement of long stones, rather than a wall. Note how the joint between two stones in the top rail is broken by the vertical pillars.

Mortar in Dry Stone Walls

Cement should not be confused with mortar. Mortar and cement should not be confused with concrete:

Cement refers to a powder, commonly OPC (ordinary Portland cement), developed in the 1820s in time for the Victorian expansion of the nation's infrastructure. Nowadays, there are several types of cement, some produced for specialized purposes, but OPC is still the one we normally associate with the term.

Mortar is a combination of aggregate (usually sand), a binding agent (lime or Portland cement) and water.

Concrete is a combination of larger aggregate, a binding agent and water.

Mortars of various types have been used for thousands of years. They seal the gap between stones and provide weatherproofing. The stone-on-stone contact is still important and is what gives a structure its main strength. Mortar assists by connecting the irregular surfaces of the stone and adding to the coefficient of friction between the surfaces. Do not think a thick mortar bed is stronger than a thin one; it is the weakest point.

Proof that stone-on-stone contact is more important than thick mortar. This Hebridean gable end was originally built with lime mortar; it contributed as much to weatherproofing as to strength. The stones were laid solidly in contact with each other, with a minimum of mortar, as it was expensive. Much of the mortar has been weathered out but the gable still stands. The core of the wall retains the hearting stone.

Cement mortars are ideal for use with brick and concrete blocks or structures made of poured concrete. They are built to be rigid and, in normal situations, unlikely to deform. Dry stone walls are made from irregular material, with no two stones the same, and they are flexible – one of its main selling points. If mortar is added, this introduces rigidity, and the wall cannot flex with the seasons. If the wall deforms it will not return to its original shape. Repairing a dry stone wall with any mortared stones is tiresome. Cutting the mortar off copestones often breaks them.

Lime-based mortars are flexible; they allow a structure to move with the seasons or settle slightly without damage.

Many hundreds of miles of stone walls were built in the 1700s. Lime or mud mortars were the available cementing options. Lime mortars might seem the obvious choice for agricultural walls but they had disadvantages, apart from the cost it added to construction.

Lime mortar is relatively simple to make but there are practical difficulties with transporting quicklime or lime putty to a remote site, finding and transporting aggregate to mix it with, and finding clean water. Lime mortars require protection from the weather until they cure. They cannot be used in frosty conditions, so walling would be difficult for at least four months of the year. Using lime mortars in the open, on a moorland, with rough stone, was not realistic.

Stone walling techniques developed to build reliable walls without mortar.

Nevertheless, mortars do have a place in dry stone walling.

A poured concrete or concrete block foundation is sometimes recommended for domestic sites, as it is a clean, dry base to build on. Engineers might see problems with this because they think a flat surface set on top of another flat surface slips too easily if subjected to some external force, such as a vehicular collision, so may specify the first course of stone is laid on a bed of soft mortar. This adds a complication.

In practical terms the friction between stone and concrete is sufficient for most purposes.

The author was once asked to build a dry stone wall 3ft (1m) high. This was the maximum height allowed under the local planning regulations. The plans called for a 12in (30cm) reinforced concrete foundation. After discussion, this was deemed to be overkill for ground that was glacial till, free-draining and solid, with no danger of frost heave. The foundation was revised and no concrete was poured, resulting in a substantial cost saving.

Individual instances are reported of mortar being used as a substitute for throughbands, with a narrow layer of mortar laid across the wall.

Mortar should always be softer than the stone. Bear this in mind when mortaring copes. Use a weak mix. The main strength should come from properly laid stone. Hard mortars have caused incalculable damage, even to important historic buildings. For more information on the proper use of traditional mortars, seek out Nigel Copsey's excellent work, detailed in the bibliography.

Mortared Copestones

Mortared copestones provide extra protection for the stonework below them. They need not look like a mass of concrete with a stone set on top; do not use mortar as an excuse for building an untidy cope. The copes should be laid on a narrow bed of mortar and be well pinned to look like any locked top. The mortar is there to assist, not dominate, the top of the wall. Having said that, bear in mind the local vernacular and the wishes of the client specifying the work.

Dealing with Trees

Dry stone walls are a natural haven for many species of plant and animal. The innocent seedling that establishes itself in the shelter of the wall may

This wall, bounding a public road, is built dry but the copes were discreetly mortared. A few copestones, at regular intervals, were not mortared, to leave some flexibility in the top of the wall. The argument for mortaring on copestones is sound: the stones are fixed properly; they can't fall on children or small animals; and are less likely to be pushed off by cattle or clambering ramblers.

Rough stonework and over-enthusiastic use of mortar spoil the appearance of what could have been a tidy piece of work. The builder assumed the strength of the wall was dependent on the mortar.

eventually grow too big and too close, unless the wall is regularly inspected and the plant is removed. If it is allowed to grow unchecked, there is every chance the roots will disturb the foundations and the trunk will push on the face of the wall as it sways in the wind. Walls and trees are not always happy neighbours.

The simplest way of dealing with a tree problem is to remove all or part of it. Cutting branches or roots could help the tree's relationship with the wall, but that might destabilize the tree and hasten its death. Removal is not a practical solution in public areas if the tree is a well-loved specimen or provides fruit or shelter. There are several alternatives.

Some answers are short-term fixes, for example rebuilding the wall across the front of the tree, actually leaning on the tree, strengthened with plenty of long stones linking the two sides of the wall. Another answer is to form a curved 'bump out' around the tree. These options save the tree and give the wall some future, but they will require frequent maintenance.

Another solution is to build wall ends right up to the tree on each side, leaving a small gap to allow the trunk to flex in the wind without hitting the stones.

These growing stems were often cut back but the roots pushed the growth and burst this mortared wall. If the tree is like this poor multi-stemmed specimen, the best solution is to take down the section of wall, remove the growth, kill the roots and rebuild the gap. Fife, Scotland.

A creative use of long stones, and a slightly leaning wall end, closes the gap between a wall and the tree. This allows the tree to grow and sway in the wind. but may not be stock-proof. Kentucky, USA.

This tree had grown next to the mortared wall, and its roots and trunk pushed and frequently caused damage. A well-built dry stone wall might have been more flexible and coped better with the movement of the tree trunk. The tree was a good specimen, one of a series, and would never be cut down. This solution was to form two wall ends, away from the influence of the tree trunk and roots, and build a wooden fence across the gap. Cawdor, Scotland.

An interesting solution to tree root damage in a mortared wall. An iron 'H' beam girder was laid as a lintel over the roots, and the area beneath the beam was built loosely enough to flex as the tree moved. Skye, Scotland.

A more refined example of how to deal with an obstruction, from Mallorca, Spain. An arch takes a retaining wall over a rock outcrop (although it could just as easily be a tree root). This is one of the strongest ways of dealing with such obstacles. The weight above the arch holds it securely in place.

The tree here is protected by a slot in the wall. This type of cavity could accommodate an existing tree or a pole, or create room for a new plant. The wall is only half wide at this point. This weakness is compensated for by stronger construction either side of the opening. The tree trunk leans on the left-hand side of the recess and the bark has 'melted' into the stones. The grey slab in the foreground is a mound in the road, a diversion for rainwater. Mallorca, Spain.

Chapter Eight

Repairing a Gap

A dry stone wall can be rebuilt from its own ruins – one of its main advantages. A good way to learn how to build walls is to have a go at 'gapping' – reconstructing a section of collapsed wall.

This section is concerned with repairs to field walls, which are usually more challenging than fixing a garden or street wall.

Many dry stone walls are over 150 years old, so repairs of some sort are inevitable. Walls should be inspected regularly to check their condition. The loss of one or two copestones will lead to further damage as the network of stone unravels. Replacing a cope in time saves eight.

Repairing a gap is not considered the high end of the craft and is sometimes dismissed as labourer's work – a quick repair to a hole in a wall that will inevitably need more attention. The skills required to do the job properly must not be underestimated, however. Gapping requires a good understanding of the principles of dry stone construction. It takes skill to reuse the stone on site, rebuild it to match the rest of the wall, and give the wall another few decades of life. Very often the stone on site is all that is available for the repair.

Gapping is a test of initiative, skill and determination. It is a chance to learn from old evidence – the stones handled by the original craftsmen.

The Ruin

A dry stone wall fails because it has been stressed, something has given way or something has collided with it. There are many opportunities for failure when a wall travels over a slope or traverses saturated moorland. Walls are often damaged at field entrances if the gateway has been hastily widened to suit modern machinery. The landowner or smallholder is frequently faced with the challenge of repairing a collapsed section of wall caused by trees, foundation failure, vehicular impact, vandalism or simple old age.

When any stone in a wall moves, it creates a gap; other stone will duly move to fill that gap. Shift leads to shift, which leads to collapse. The damage could be a total failure of many yards, which needs taking down to the foundation; or it could be a small section, say copestones and one or two courses, which could be stripped down and repaired in an hour. Repairing gaps on flat ground is straightforward. A collapsed section in a 6ft-high (1.8m) wall running across a slope on boggy moorland has its own challenges.

At first sight, the problem is daunting: there is a pile of stone in chaotic order, trickled down a slope, sunk into the ground, into long grass and muddy water.

The task is simplified if we go through a sequence of sorting and foundation repair.

Stripping out and Sorting

Stripping the collapse down to the foundation reveals why the wall failed and suggests how it could be rebuilt stronger.

Clear away bushes, tall grass, weeds, old machinery – anything in the way. If the gap has been there for some time, there may be a 'farmer's fix', such as an old gate or pallet, maybe a temporary post and wire

This damage started as a few loose copestones, knocked off by jumping deer. Over time more stones were pushed over. The throughstone, lying in the middle, became a launching pad into the other side of the dyke.

fence. All this must be removed to get easier access to the site.

If there is livestock in the field, and the work will take more than the day, erect some sort of temporary fencing to protect the work site and keep the animals from escaping.

Wear gloves when dismantling an old wall, as the stone will be rough, and keep an eye out for sharp metal. On hill dykes, watch out for glass and hypodermic needles. In sheep country, in the days before pregnant ewes were inoculated, and lambing was on the open hill, the shepherds inoculated lambs after birth. When the vaccine bottle was empty, it was, often as not, stuffed in a hole in a dyke. Cartridge cases, old unidentified iron and wire find their way there too. Some of these items were put there by the original dykers. Mummified mice and rabbits are also often found inside a wall.

Leave a passageway a couple of feet wide at each side of the wall to work from. That reduces the chance of tripping up.

Dismantle the pile of fallen stone carefully; try to avoid any more collapse. Listen carefully for the dry, grinding sound of moving stone. Make sure there is an escape route if stone starts to fall. If you can do it safely, remove a few copestones beyond the ends of

the gap; this takes some weight off and reduces the chance of more collapse.

The overlapping nature of stones in a wall means dismantling can go further than first intended. Take the wall back only as far as necessary, to where it is still strong and standing. At some point you have to make the decision to accept the wall as it is, for all its faults, and get on with repairing the gap.

If many yards of wall start to unravel, the owner must start to question whether the cost of repair justifies the work. Should it be replaced with other types of fencing?

All the stone for the rebuild should be in the collapsed heap, unless it happened some time ago and stone was carted away for other purposes. From previous sections, we know a free-standing dry stone wall consists of various shapes and sizes of stone, some with a specialized purpose. We must sort the stones in the pile according to the job they do.

If the wall collapsed recently, the stones will still have a patina of lichens and mosses indicating which side faced out. The top side of these stones is dirty with cobwebs and dust; the underside is cleaner and dry. These indicators speed up the rebuilding process since fewer decisions have to be made about how to place each stone.

A well-placed throughstone did its job – stopping the damage from travelling far. If there is a chance of it moving while the repair is ongoing, leave some stones under it to act as a temporary support. They can be removed when the repair gets up to that height.

The stones were handled and shaped by the original waller. His way of placing a particular stone is usually still valid. Sometimes, though, they were not the best choices, and contributed to the failure of the wall. If, for example, a lot of stones were laid traced or on edge, that will have to be corrected. Extra stone may be required on site.

Copestones, coverstones and throughstones are somewhere in the pile, if they were ever in the original wall. They are identifiable by their shape, size and patina, and should be carefully set aside. Their purpose is specialized. Do not use these stones for basic building. They might not be easy to replace. This is a repair, so assume there will only be enough stone on site for the rebuild.

Bring some specialist stone onto the site if the original design needs improvement. A few more throughstones will add considerably to the wall's strength and stability.

The hearting stones are usually clean, with little or no patina. Set them carefully aside in a few piles on either side of the gap, ready for reuse. Often the hearting has 'disappeared' because it was never there in the first place. The wall may have flexed because it was not built tight enough, and the hearting fell down among the foundation. There is a chance the original wallers skimped and left the interior of the wall comparatively hollow. Some hill dykes were never hearted to the standard we have today simply because smaller stone was not available and the rough face stones bound together well enough.

Save flat pieces or long thin pieces in a special place. They are useful for small gaps or as shims, especially nearer the top of the wall.

Don't throw stone far from where it is needed. Keep the site tidy.

Lay the building stones out, about half on each side of the gap. If the wall runs across a slope, move the copes and heavy stones on to the top side. This saves the exertion of having to carry them up a slope, then lifting them on top of the wall. Think ahead to avoid creating unnecessary work.

Some wallers like to organize the stone into various sizes, in different piles. Sorting does not need to be a lot of work; simply spread out the stone so everything is visible. The pile of small rubble left at the end of the repair could be hiding the flat stone you needed halfway up the wall.

The foundation stones are at the bottom of the collapse. They are often big, 'ugly' stones dug into the earth. Clear small stones and loose soil away from around them and check why they moved. If the foundation looks sound, don't disturb it.

The site is now clear and tidy, ready for rebuilding.

Repairing a Free-Standing Section

In the top image the site has been cleared for the repair. From this angle, it may look chaotic but the dyker is experienced and knows where everything is. String lines have been set across the open space. Buckets are ready for the hearting.

The face stones are clearly visible in the pile, along with some longer, flatter, ones. They may be throughstones.

In the bottom image the work is completed. The copestones are most likely the originals because they are the right size and moss-covered. There are no coverstones. The repair merges nicely with the original wall. Stones are laid level. There are no unnecessary small stones or chinking in the face. Note the good bonding – 'one over two, two over one'. Largest stones are at the bottom, smaller ones towards the top, where they were needed to get the top line of the double ready and level for the copestones.

Repairing a free-standing section. Work by Drystone Walling Perthshire.

Lines and Frames

String lines are still useful when repairing a gap, unless it is a short section where the line of the wall and the batter are easily judged by eye.

The collapsed section usually sits between two racked-back ends, the sloping back sections of wall, which remain standing. They represent a cross-section of the wall, giving the dimensions for reconstruction. Stretch a line, on steel pins, from one end of the gap to the other. If the wall has moved out of shape at either end of the gap, try to correct that without causing more damage. It is cheaper, in terms of time and effort, to accept the distortion, adjust the string line and built accordingly.

Four lengths of rebar hammered into the ground on each side, and on each end of the gap, will also indicate the profile of the wall.

As with a new build, the lines are raised occasionally to guide the builder. This helps keep the stones horizontal and the courses reasonably level.

Frames get in the way, unless the gap is a long stretch and totally stripped out.

Preparing for the Rebuild

The collapse may have exposed a fault in the wall. We now have the chance to eliminate the fault and replace it with stronger work. If the damage was caused by tree roots or water, this is the time to build in a proper opening, widen the foundation or introduce some bigger, longer, stones to strengthen the wall.

In most cases, the waller is limited to the stones on site. If the gap is a big one, it is worth a reconnaissance before starting, to check what is there. Is more stone required? What type of stone is in short supply? How can it be brought to site?

If the section has been repaired before, there might be a pile of extra stone nearby, suggesting the last waller skimped on the repair. Maybe they rebuilt the wall slimmer or lower. Scout the area for any copes or face stones that rolled away, and check out the possibility of garnering hearting stone from nearby sources.

Repairing the Wall from the Ground up

The Foundation

Most wall collapses are a result of a failed foundation. Foundation stones are the bottom layer of a wall and support the weight above. They may have slipped due to undermining by moles or rabbits. They may have moved because they were laid on a slope. The weight of a snowdrift may have pushed them over, or water accumulated in the back and softened the ground. Ploughing too near the wall may have undermined them. If a foundation stone moves, the stones above are obliged to follow.

There are two main options if large foundation stones have slipped. If they have sunk into the ground or moved slightly to one side but feel solid, accept the situation and build over the top of them. If a foundation stone is still mobile, it must be stabilized and brought into line. If it is big, dig out the soil behind it and lever it back with a pinch bar. There is no harm in a solidly set foundation stone sitting a little out from the face of the wall. In a moorland wall this is not unattractive; just take care it does not provide a step for an ambitious sheep. In a formal garden wall, the homeowner could be persuaded to accept this projection because it adds charm and visual interest.

Another, harder, option for a wayward foundation stone is to replace it, or break it up with a large hammer.

If the foundation course is large and irregular, spend some time levelling out the coursing with smaller stone. This establishes a relatively flat surface on which to build.

Other options to consider when rebuilding the foundation include:

- Stepping the foundation, like a staircase, when moving up or along a slope. This keeps stones horizontally level and reduces the chance of slippage.

- Setting stones on edge. A couple of long stones laid on edge across, or part way across, the width of the foundation might be stronger than smaller stones laid flat. The edged stone bites into the ground.
- Importing large stones for a stronger foundation, especially in soft ground.
- Building a section of single wall to get over a dip in the ground.
- Putting in a scarcement for a bigger foundation footprint, and stability.
- Avoiding a really awkward spot all together by constructing two wall ends, one on each side, and fencing the gap with post and wire.
- Improving the local drainage by incorporating an opening to allow water a free passage.

The Double – First Lift

The rules for laying stones for a repair are exactly the same as for building a new wall. Lay the stones level, with their longest edge into the centre of the wall. Break the joints. Ensure the hearting is filled up.

The stone supply is limited and specific, so use all stones carefully.

Try to keep the stonework style and appearance consistent with the walling on each side of the gap, but do not compromise on strength.

Don't rebuild the wall narrower than it originally was. If necessary, build wider for strength, even though this may need more stone.

Check progress from time to time by stepping back (carefully) for an inspection of bonding and coursing.

The Throughstones

At halfway, or whatever the local pattern is, place the throughstone(s), pin them securely and avoid running joints up each side. If the original throughstones have broken, use the two pieces, reaching in from each side and interlinking in the middle, to perform the same task.

If there are no throughstones (a likely cause of the collapse), find the most suitable stones in the pile and use them. If necessary, bring in suitable throughstones for the next day's work. Although it's a bother, attention to detail pays dividends. An extra set or two of throughstones strengthens the wall.

If most of the stone in the wall is long pieces, interlinking in the middle, there may never have been formal throughstones. The original wallers used what was on site to get the best result. They made sure the stones interlinked in the middle and saw less need for conventional throughstones. In such situations it should be possible to rebuild the wall following the original wallers' processes. That, of course, assumes the 1860s wallers did good work: if they cut corners, that must be corrected now.

The Double – Second Lift

Continue the repair up through the courses until both outer faces of stone, properly hearted, are level with the double on either side of the collapse.

There may be (hopefully only mild) panic as the work gets near the end. Is there enough stone?

When the double is completed, make sure that it is well hearted, that the stones in the top course are secure and that none are laid traced. The top of the double must be secure enough to hold the weight of the coverstones and copestones.

Covers and Copes

It will now be safe to remove a few copestones on either side of the gap, if this has not already been done, as there is far less chance of further collapse. Dismantling the cope for a few feet on either side of the repair means the rebuilt cope will extend smoothly over and beyond the gap. It will have a nicer top line and draw less attention to the repair.

Set the coverstones and/or copestones to match the existing. Stretch a line over the top of the existing copestones on each side of the gap and lay the copestones to that height. Lift short copes with a small flat stone if necessary. Once the copestones have been set, lightly hammer shims between them to tighten them and create the locked top.

Tidy Up

At the end of the process, tidy up. Each stone left on the grass is one mouthful less for a hungry ewe. Take away the bed end, gate, pallet, tangled wire – whatever was filling the gap.

The ground that was under the collapsed stone soon recovers, and there will be a flush of new grass. Minerals from the broken stone, along with the compaction and disturbance of the ground, stimulate growth.

Repairing a partly retaining wall, a collapsed section of dry stone dyke. On the right-hand side, the racked-back section shows the original profile. The hearting is clearly visible. The face stones are large and must be lifted some distance to get them into the wall. The hearting and earth in the retaining part might fall into the wall as it is dismantled. If the loose material is not in the way, leave it hanging there. Work around it until the rebuild gets to that level, then dismantle it carefully. Work by Drystone Walling Perthshire.

A completed repair. This repair, of damage seen in the previous image, ties in well with the old dyke. Any bumps and lumps in the section of wall that did not collapse were accepted, made strong and built over. The main purpose of the job was to repair the gap, not the whole dyke. A scarcement made from the largest boulders secures the base. The stones have been graded, with the largest at the bottom and smaller ones towards the top. The repair is under trees and will soon 'green up' in the relatively damp shade. Work by Drystone Walling Perthshire.

Building back stronger. The upper image shows a collapse, partly cleared, beyond the margins of the original collapse. The lower image records the repair. The condition of the old wall has been accepted and the repair merged in with the old stonework. The foundation was built stronger, with the biggest stones, and brought up to a level to provide a good base for the flatter stones in the upper courses. Note how the course of stones under the cope is flat and level, obviously guided by a line. The copestones are well chosen – a mix of the originals and others selected from the ruin. The yellow line is a folding ruler. Work by Drystone Walling Perthshire.

This section of Kentucky wall was a rebuild, using the original old limestone. The stone is friable and tends to break when the wall is dismantled. Despite that, the waller built a clean, uncluttered face, pleasing to the eye, with a minimum of small chips and pinnings.

Chapter Nine

Retaining Walls

Trautwine's excellent 1937 edition of *The Civil Engineer's Reference Book* (details in the bibliography) provided some information on this topic. His observations have been overtaken by more recent scientific experiments, but the essence of them is still repeated in modern publications.

A retaining wall holds something back, faces something up or resists the force of a moveable slope – sometimes all three at once.

Retaining walls exist in various forms all over the world, as part of extensive agricultural systems. Chinese rice paddies, ancient Peruvian cultivation terraces, Austrian vineyards and Spanish olive groves all follow a basic pattern of 'stair stepping' the slope. Retaining walls in the Himalayan foothills hold up roads and railway tracks.

The Victorians built thousands of retaining walls as part of the nation's road, rail and canal infrastructure. Many of these were built dry and have been unsympathetically 'repaired' with concrete. This often restricts their inbuilt flexibility and leads to more problems than it solves (O'Reilly and Perry, 2009).

For most ordinary domestic situations, even most agricultural ones, a retaining wall is seldom over 6ft (1.8m) high. It establishes a hard edge to hold up a flower bed or support a driveway. The building of a retaining wall usually incorporates a reduction in the angle of the slope on the upside and the creation of a useful flat area on the downhill side. For some landscaping, it is far easier to form the ground into a slope and compact it.

A low retaining wall cutting into, and built across, a slope slows down water. It soaks into the ground rather than scouring the topsoil away. A piece of stable ground is created that supports plant growth. This becomes a self-sustaining cycle, often employed in revitalizing arid land and as part of permaculture systems in, among other places, sub-Saharan Africa and North America.

The theory of retaining walls also applies to something as simple as a raised planting bed. We could think of these as 'containing walls' because they surround, contain and support a piece of ground.

The recommended dimensions for retaining walls vary. There are many modern engineering inputs into the science of these walls, advocating various angles and proportions, depending on the pressures, actual or anticipated, behind the wall. The forces behind a retaining wall are complex. Any movement across, or along, the ground held up by a retaining wall creates a bow wave of pressure. The passage of one large vehicle will have little effect, but the designers must allow for the cumulative effect of hundreds, over time.

Trautwine provides the ultimate answer: 'Experience, rather than theory, must be our guide ...'. In other words, consult a local expert, someone with a proven portfolio.

Trautwine tells us the width of the foundation should be up to half of the height of the wall. Higher walls therefore mean wider foundations. This, of course, defines the amount and type of stone required. Wider walls need more face stones and longer stones (to reach well behind the face of the wall), and more stone for the backfill. There is no harm in making a retaining wall wider. This adds to the cost of labour and material but, if properly built, reduces the chance of failure.

Typical retaining walls in Mallorca, Spain, incorporating the native rock in the foundations, with cobbled pathways for access up a slope. Many miles of retaining walls support planting areas for fruit and olive trees. The large stones in the foundation jut out from the original rocky slope. They provide an anchor point for the foundation and add some visual interest to the coursed stonework.

It is best to design the wall and then look for stone. Do not design a wall based on how much stone is immediately available.

In the twenty-first century, local authority regulations often limit the height of a retaining wall. Engineering guidance is advisable for any large-scale retaining wall, certainly for walls over 5ft (1.5m), or those intended to hold back loose material or support a live load, such as a roadway or car park.

Retaining walls come under many names, including 'gravity walls', 'breast walls' or 'face walls'. Each of these terms has a specific meaning within its field. For our purposes, it is enough to understand that a retaining wall should be wide, massive and bulky. One hundred tons of rock piled in front of a slope will hold it back. We naturally prefer something that looks more elegant, with a bit more design input. A properly built wall using 40 tons will do the same job and takes up less space.

Basic Types of Dry Stone Retaining Wall

Dry stone retaining walls come in a few basic types, with a myriad of local variations, depending on the local stone and the purpose of the wall.

Free-Standing Wall in Front of the Slope

Bearing in mind that the width of the foundation should be half the total height of the wall, aim for a batter of one in six; that's a reasonable ratio that works for most walls and most stone types.

A 5ft-high (1.5m) wall will therefore be 2.5ft (75cm) wide at the bottom. The width at the top will depend on how the retaining wall relates to the banking behind.

The wall is constructed as normal, immediately in front of the slope, often with a more substantial foundation and more throughstones to add strength. The aim is to create a solid mass of stone. The wall's batter and the cut-back slope form up a 'V' of empty space. This void is eventually packed with solid stone and hearting, which binds together and gets tighter if pressure increases from behind.

The public face of any type of retaining wall should be as neat as any other wall. The back side of the wall remains hidden against the ground it supports, so can be rougher, even of a different material. Aim for strength rather than elegance at the back. Never compromise on strength. The aim is to produce something to resist the forces behind, and allow for unforeseen circumstances.

In the world of dry stone, this means building solid, heavy and strong.

After completing each course, packing the inside of the wall solidly with hearting, and filling up the space between the wall and the slope with clean stone, the background soil is pulled down and compacted into what little space remains. This entirely eliminates voids and means there is a minimum of small material in the body of the wall. The aim is to pack the space solidly, using no material that can move, or be squeezed or washed out.

Do not fill the space behind a retaining wall with mostly earth or any type of gravel. The latter is good for paths, but not in or behind any type of wall. Small rounded material, such as pea gravel, must never be used in a retaining wall. It acts like ball bearings between the larger stones, reducing friction and encouraging movement, especially if the build quality is also second rate.

Earth is a poor infill for several reasons. It can change easily from firm, dry material to highly mobile mud. Rock is more reliable; it is heavier than soil and adds considerably more to the wall's mass. This increases the wall's strength and its ability to resist forces from behind.

Single-Faced Wall Against a Slope

Consider this as a double-faced wall cut down the middle. It is, in effect, one face of stone laid against a slope using as many long stones as possible to connect the face of the wall with the earth banking behind the wall.

Some authorities on the subject call this a 'face wall' rather than a retaining wall as it is built to clad and protect a slope; they reserve the term 'retaining wall' for a much more substantial structure that has to resist moveable forces from behind.

The foundation's width, once again, follows Trautwine's recommendation to be about half the height of the wall with a batter of around one in six.

Just like the free-standing retaining wall, the ground behind the stone is pulled down carefully after completing each course and filling the back space with the maximum amount of hearting and clean stone. The amount of non-stone material should be kept to a minimum.

When it comes to the top few inches, it is reasonable to put in soil or mulch if planting is intended on that edge.

This single-faced retaining wall was just over 5ft (1.5m) high when completed. It faces up a cut into stable glacial till. The first course above ground level was 3ft (90cm) from the base of the cut. The build included many long stones to make the vital link between the front of the wall and the face of the slope. The design had two or three of these long stones every square yard. This created massive strength, particularly in the bottom half of the wall. String lines were stretched between two lengths of rebar, one at each end of the section. The batter was approximately one in six.

Single Wall, Hard Against a Slope

This is an efficient way of creating a one-stone-wide wall to hold back a slope. The size of the stones means they are usually placed by machine and a team who guide the process with prybars. This version is especially suitable for large-scale walls that aim to mimic a natural landscape. They look more attractive as they weather and plant growth becomes established. The space behind these large stones must be packed solid with smaller stones to stop earth from finding its way through.

A section of retaining wall nears completion. Larger stones protect the unfinished edge. The wall shields the slope and provides an attractive boundary feature. Once grass was established, no soil or water washed over the stones, or ever came through from the back. The sandy soil was free-draining; no formal drainage was incorporated. If there had been a water problem, a perforated pipe would have been built deep into the foundation to catch water and lead it away to one end. No fabric was used behind the wall. It was certainly not required with such a compacted slope.

This wall borders a change of levels in a public garden. The stones fit reasonably tightly together, leaving room for vegetation – some deliberately planted. Seattle, USA.

Veneer Against a Concrete or Block Wall

This fourth option is a more substantial structure, which might be advocated by civil engineers. It is a hybrid combining the strength of a reinforced concrete wall with the aesthetics of a natural stone face. The stone could be discreetly mortared to the concrete or built dry. This type of solid barrier requires a proper drainage plan. Regular openings in a long wall are preferable to one long drain at the back, leading water away to one end or the other.

Using Lines and Frames

Setting the A-frames and string lines for a retaining wall is straightforward.

If it is built as a free-standing wall, the A-frames are set in front of the banking and the lines are used as normal.

When the retaining wall is built as a single-faced wall against the slope, the line and batter of the wall are usually established by a piece of timber or rebar, one at each end (for a straight wall), braced from the top of the slope. One line, stretched between these straight edges, defines the front face of the wall. Like with any other wall, this line is raised with each course of stones.

For a single-faced retaining wall, the back face, nearest the banking, does not require a string line unless and until it eventually rises to become a low wall above ground level. If that is the intention, the build should be solid and wide enough to support the stonework at the top of the wall. Once the retaining wall emerges as a free-standing wall, above ground level, a frame and lines for the back of the wall can be set.

Foundations

Retaining walls are often built across a slope. This could make laying the foundation tricky, but the principles of a foundation for a free-standing wall still apply. It should be 'stepped' up the slope so that the stones can be laid truly horizontal.

Use the biggest stones at the bottom. If there are enough of them, and they are of comparable size, set them up as a scarcement, jutting out a few inches from the main wall. This adds stability and is a nice architectural feature. If the large stones vary in size, dig out the ground underneath them to level them off and create a relatively flat surface on which to build.

French wallers lay the foundation stones for a retaining wall perpendicular to the face – at right angles to the angle of batter. The stones in the face of the wall are also laid perpendicular to the batter. The inner tails of long stones slope down into the centre of the wall, where they are held solidly by the weight of the stones above. If the centre of the wall is pushed up, the wall's weight resists the upthrust. When the upward force subsides, the stones settle back down again. Laying the stones this way adds to the stability and reduces the effects of undermining. This inclination of the stones is especially advantageous in areas susceptible to frost heave or seismic activity.

If a retaining wall is built anywhere where there is likely to be a seasonal flow of water, consider building a lunky (*see* Chapter 10) into the foundation or setting large foundation stones a few inches apart to form a natural-looking drainage channel. The importance of drainages, especially when associated with frost heave, is discussed below.

Topping Off

A retaining wall can be topped off like a free-standing wall – with flat capstones, vertical copestones, or something as simple as soil pulled down to meet the top course of stones. The top stones should be laid securely, or even discreetly mortared for added safety. If it is intended to plant along the top of the wall, the copestones should be solidly set, with sufficient depth of topsoil behind them.

Frost Heave and the Need for Drainage

Frost heave is caused by the expansion of the ground as water freezes, by approximately 8–10 per cent. This is not generally a problem in Europe but must be anticipated in parts of North America. Freezing soil means a retaining wall is vulnerable to ground movement in the foundation and from the soil behind. One general remedy for this threat is to control the water. This requires extra attention to drainage and build quality, with the aim of allowing the structure to flex without bursting.

Retaining walls are free-draining, in that water flows through them both vertically and horizontally. The Victorians, and previous generations of engineers, did not have plastic piping, so relied on the universal principle of gravity to assist drainage.

There is a danger that the foundation trench can become a basin where water gathers, therefore it must have a way of safely draining away before it freezes.

In most cases, especially when the retaining wall is only 3 or 4ft (1–1.2m) high, and there is no obvious flow of water during construction, the wall can drain itself. If there is a chance of increased water flow, perhaps over the winter months, a perforated pipe laid behind the wall, below the level of a strongly built foundation, can lead water away to a drain. A perforated pipe is no use if it sits immediately behind the wall above the level of the foundation stones: water finds its way to the lowest point and that's where the drain needs to be.

There are low-tech alternatives to plastic or clay pipe. A foundation trench with carefully built stones and a few inches of well-tamped angular gravel can act as the drainage channel. The trench leads to one end, to where a more conventional drain can take the water away.

If necessary, a surface drain further up the slope, or some distance behind the retaining wall, can catch and divert water before it poses any danger to the wall.

Solid and free-draining – a Mallorcan retaining wall with water pouring through it. The wall is 8.2ft (2.5m) high with 30 tons of compacted stone in the back. It is a restoration of a section that repeatedly failed. Note the two vertically set columns of stone, called *capginyes*. They provide stability and separate the old work from the new. LLUC MIR ANGUERA

Fabric

Do not use geotextile, landscaping fabric or the like behind the wall, thinking it will stop soil from coming through, prevent solids from blocking the permeability of the stones, or add to the strength of the structure. The fabric will clog before the stonework and add unnecessary pressure to the back if the wall. It could be a monster waiting to bite back. Apart from the expense and extra work required for a material, which might be badly installed, there is the problem of introducing degradable plastics into the soil and leaving an inconvenience for the future, if the wall ever needs repair or the ground digging for planting. If some kind of barrier is judged to be necessary, a compacted vertical layer of thin lawn turf, clay or straw could do the same job more cheaply and with less inconvenience.

A combination of fabric and gravel is especially lethal, as it introduces extra pressure to the back of a wall. Gravel is a pile of ball bearings trying to flatten itself out, and this force is amplified if it presses onto a restraining fabric. The only place for gravel is flat on the ground, where it might be useful for drainage or to firm up the surface.

Budget, space and time may be limiting factors; fabric is no substitute for solid material used properly.

If soil does wash through, something is wrong with the drainage or, more than likely, the wall is not wide enough. If a retaining wall is built wide, and is well packed at the back with solidly placed stone, nothing should percolate through to the front. Water and any loose soil should fall down through the stonework well before it reaches the face of the wall.

A Final Thought

The author has noticed a particular problem with retaining walls in North America, particularly garden retaining walls around 2–3ft (0.6–1m) high. Stone is expensive. It is therefore often laid traced and on edge to get maximum amount of face area from a load of stone. The walls are frequently only one stone thick, backed up with compost. This makes for weak construction that is vulnerable to failure when knocked or pushed. There is no reason why the back of such a wall could not be built with cheaper stone, even broken concrete – the back of the wall is forever invisible.

Chapter Ten

Openings, Arches and Roofs

Openings Through a Wall

If a waller knows how to build a length of wall and a wall end, and knows how to put in a lintel, it is a logical next step to rearrange these components into a variety of structures.

The Lunky

These handy openings are also known as smoos, smoots and hogg holes (where 'hogg' refers to a young sheep rather than a pig).

The lunky comes in various shapes and sizes. Larger ones allow sheep or lambs through and stop cows. Smaller ones were used for trapping rabbits or hares. They were often built at regular intervals along a boundary wall between two neighbouring estates. This allowed shepherds to move stray sheep back to the right side of the wall without having to travel far for a gate.

The component parts are easy to understand. A lunky consist of two low sections of wall end with one or two long stones (lintels) laid across the top – in effect a stone casing similar to that for a door. The lintels should have a solid 'bite' into the stonework on either side of the gap, at least a few inches. Once the lintel is in place, the stonework for the wall continues over the top as normal. A flat stone, a padstone, in the floor of the opening keeps the passage from deteriorating into a muddy trench and undermining the sides.

A lunky takes less effort to build than two full-size wall ends with a gate and gateposts and is less likely to get damaged. The opening is easily blocked (and unblocked) with a pile of stones, a flagstone or, in modern times, a pallet.

An excellent example of a lunky. Note the vertical sides, the padstone and the 'bite' of the lintel into the well-coursed stonework. Work by Jared Flynn.

Lintelled openings are also useful for taking a wall over water or tree roots, and can be adapted to make shelves, niches, alcoves or openings in a wall for any purpose. The basic design of a lunky is also adjustable to give access to buried cables or drainage pipes, an important consideration for uncomplicated repair or renewal of these services.

Another form of opening is two vertical slabs set a short distance apart, just wide enough for a person – but not livestock – to squeeze through, hence its

A pass-through for sheep. Roscommon, Ireland.

A water gate. The wall ends at each side of the stream, and a pier in the middle support lintels carrying a dyke across. Assynt, Scotland.

This site does not have stone long enough for lintels. A wall head on each side of the stream suspends a gate over the watercourse. The luxurious moss growth tells us the banks of this stream are damp and sheltered. Southwest Scotland.

An Irish example of a lunky. The local limestone is easily fabricated, almost like timber. Two thick slabs, on edge, form the sides. Another long thick slab forms the lintel. This exhibits the best use of the local rock type; don't break a long stone or a slab unless you absolutely have to. Aran Islands, Ireland.

This gateway is built from western Irish limestone, a versatile material easily formed into posts and slabs. The smaller opening is temporarily blocked with small stone. The larger opening is further enclosed within two wall ends. The whole central section can be dismantled and quickly replaced if something bigger must get through.

This squeeze-through stile is made from upright slabs of limestone. The Burren, Ireland.

name, a 'squeeze stile'. This narrow opening could also be built as two wall ends set close together.

Lintelled Openings, off the Ground and Upside Down

A lintelled opening can be built, in effect, upside down to create an opening in the upper part of a wall – a stile. A flat stone like a coverband is laid on top of a section of double. Two wall ends are formed at each side of the gap up to copestone height. Solid copestones are set on each side of the gap. If the passageway is high up in the wall, throughstones, protruding a foot or more on both sides, make steps, and a stock-proof way for people to get up and across the wall while excluding all animals except agile dogs.

A stile through an Irish dry stone wall, assisted with mortar, as befits a well-used passageway. The narrow gap inhibits passage of livestock, allowing one man and his dog free access. Note the padstone at grass level, where everyone steps. The top stone in the middle of the gap is a narrow blade, set on edge to separate the two sides. Projecting stones on the other side take the traveller back down to ground level.

This stile, into a field in Inis Oirr, Ireland, clearly shows its similarity to an upside-down lunky. Jutting stones aid access through the gap.

A Bee Bole

A bee bole is a sheltering alcove for an old-fashioned bee skep. Basically it is a lunky built off the ground, part way up the wall. The sides of this opening are vertical, with stone laid as for a wall end. The top of the opening is a lintel made from two wide slabs of slate, and the back and floor of the opening are formed from slate slabs. This design could be adapted for many other purposes. In the picture, the near-vertical line on the left is a joint between this section of wall and another type of wall.

A bee bole, a recess for a bee skep. Dry Stone Walling Association collection, Cumbria, England.

Arches

An arch is a curved structure that reaches up and over. It is an efficient way of achieving height and distance without the use of lintels or supporting pillars. An arch is strong but relatively delicate – an upward thrust could disrupt it.

We are familiar with arches from their use in bridges and cathedrals. An arch can also be one stone wide, as an ornamental opening into a garden or as narrow as the width of a dry stone wall. Moon gates are another kind of arched opening – effectively an arch with another arch built upside down under it to create a circle.

The mechanics and physics of arches can get complicated. For us, it is enough to understand an arch stays in place because its weight, and the weight above it, pushes down. The individual stones in the arch absorb the stress and that downward thrust is opposed by solid abutments on either side. If the walls to the side of an arch fail, the arch will also fail.

The shaped stones around the open rim of the arch are called voussoirs or ring stones. These stones are shaped to fit tightly together, with as much surface-to-surface contact as possible, to evenly transfer the forces within the arch. If it is difficult to shape voussoirs, or they do not fit tightly, slide thin stones between them to fill the space. The work should look symmetrical and tidy.

Rough stones can be fitted together to form an arch, although this would rely on brute force to hold the ring together rather than the finessed grace of shaped stone.

The simplest arch is a semicircle. Straight lines from the centre of each slanted voussoir would meet at an imaginary point, the centre of the complete circle. This is the same application of geometry as used in the construction of walls on a curve. A line from a central point defines the extent of the curve and how each stone relates to the curve.

During construction, the stonework of an arch is fairly delicate. The stones are laid perpendicular to the curve, supported by a wooden frame called falsework. The falsework for a one-stone-wide garden arch will be as narrow as the individual stones, whereas the falsework for a bridge extends all the way across and along the underside of the bridge.

The falsework must be specially fabricated for bridges or arches. For small openings, any round object could be used for a support – a bucket, an oil drum, even a car tyre. Just make sure the shape can

be removed when the arch is completed. If a wooden falsework or bucket is supported by a few removable wedges, this gives it somewhere to drop into, making it easier to get out. Hard-packed mounds of earth and turf have also been used as supporting frames for small arches.

The voussoir in the top middle of an arch is called the keystone. It is put in last, to lock the other voussoirs in place. It must be shaped carefully for maximum contact with the stones on either side. This solid contact ensures all the forces in the arch are contained and equally distributed down through the ring stones. Do not make the keystone from a softer stone than the rest of the arch; the strain on it may cause damage and failure. The keystone must be a tight fit but not so tight that it pushes the other stones aside when it is laid. Once the keystone connects and solidifies the ring, the arch is self-supporting.

In the case of a bridge vault, all the stones across the width of the span, and from end to end of the span, are laid on edge onto the falsework – the wooden frame carefully shaped to form the curve of the arch. Once the voussoirs, the keystones and all the other stones are fitted across the width of the bridge, they

A nearly completed arch in a super-tight wall. This is a more complex arch shape than the semicircular arch. Ring stones sit on the falsework. The voussoirs are fitted the same way, once the falsework is designed. When the final stone, the keystone, is set, it holds the ring stones tight. The forces within the arch go down to the side walls. Strong side walls are necessary to resist the forces within any arch. Work by John Bland.

are tightened with smaller stones to lock the arch. The framework can then be safely removed.

The abutments to each side of any arch are built up at the same time as the voussoirs. This puts weight against the developing arch and prevents the ring of stones from distorting.

In the case of an arched opening, once the keystone is in place and the abutting stonework is brought up to full height, the falsework can be safely removed.

This is always an anxious moment. Providing the voussoirs are properly installed, and the stonework to each side is strong enough to resist the simultaneous downward and outward thrust of the arch, all should be well.

When an arch for a bridge is completed, the deck of the bridge (the top side of the arch's curve) can be flattened off with paving. Parapets and embankments add the final touches for a viable path or roadway.

Small-scale arches have many applications in dry stone walls. This simple, elegant, semicircular arch of Mallorcan limestone uses exactly the same techniques as larger arches. The uprights on either side of the water trough are built vertically. The fourth course of stones above the trough are springers – the ring stones 'spring' from them. The keystone has clearly been shaped for the purpose.

Kay's Drystone Bridge, Ontario, Canada. The ring stones of the arch sits solidly against the abutment. They were shaped and laid out in advance, before fitting on the falsework. Metal brackets for the handrail were fitted into the stonework during construction. The bridge deck was covered with pitched stone – stone laid tight, side to side, long edge down. This 12ft-span (3.6m) dry stone bridge was built by John Shaw-Rimmington and a group of wallers from Canada, the USA, Ireland and Australia in 2010.

An arched opening built through a dry stone wall. The arch curve starts at foundation level, laid on top of a wooden support – the falsework. Thin pieces of stone between individual voussoirs ensure they make a tidy and symmetrical curve. This opening coincides with a dip in the ground, which guides water towards a drain. Such an opening could also deal with tree roots. Kentucky, USA.

Removing the framework from beneath a completed arch for a dry stone bridge in Perth, Ontario, Canada. The bridge was built by wallers and masons from Canada, Scotland, Ireland and the USA as part of Perth's 200th anniversary celebrations in 2016.

A Moon Gate

These circular openings are based on a feature from ancient Chinese architecture. In the example shown here, note how the voussoir stones radiate from an imaginary centre point and the shape of the circle is held in place by the mass of horizontal walling on each side. The bottom half of the circular opening is created by laying stone carefully, according to a framework. When the stonework gets up to halfway, the frame is flipped. While building proceeds on the upper part of the ring of the arch, the stonework on either side of the opening is also brought up. The keystone (the one at top middle) is inserted last.

For safety in this type of mixed stone construction, the falsework is best left in place until all work is done.

A moon gate, built by members and friends of Drystone Canada. Designed by Eric Landman. The metalwork, by Dan Sinclair, is called 'The Windswept Tree'.

Putting on a Roof

We have learned enough from previous chapters to create a curved wall with rounded corners or a rectangle with squared corners. The techniques for building wall ends and a lunky can be adapted to create a doorway. It seems reasonable to progress towards roofing a small dry stone structure, perhaps for use as a root cellar or animal housing, or even as a modern 'eco-house'. Such a structure could be recessed into a slope, using the techniques discussed for retaining walls.

Hebridean Blackhouse

The Hebridean blackhouse is an excellent example of a comparatively easily built dry stone structure. It is a version of a type (the North Atlantic longhouse) that spread with the Norse expansion from Scandinavia to North America. Earlier versions were built of turf and wood. This stone-built version dates back to the early 1800s and is still a common sight in the Scottish Hebrides, though very few are actually used as housing.

This structure could be described as a lidless stone box with one or two openings for windows, and a doorway. The walls are topped off with a timber-framed roof and, originally, thatch.

Typical external measurements, for the stonework, from a blackhouse rebuilt at the Highland Folk Museum in Newtonmore, Scotland, are 16m long × 6m wide × 1.6m high with walls 1.4m thick (approximately 53ft × 20ft × 5ft with walls 5ft thick). The internal space is not wide and is well insulated by the thick walls.

Two thick outer faces of stone are built up using the basic dry stone construction principles, guided by frames and string lines. The centre of the wall is filled with earth and rubble, and packed hard. As many long stones as possible are laid from the outer faces into the middle of the wall. With such a thick wall, normal throughstones are not practical. The walls are slightly battered on the outer face and vertical on the inner face. The corners are rounded on the outside and square on the inside.

The walls are brought up to height and levelled off. A competent carpenter should then be able to build on a frame for the thatched roof. The roof is fully supported by the stone walls and substantially increases the headroom within the blackhouse.

If such a structure was intended as a dwelling house it would, of course, have to pass the local planning regulations, and be built by an experienced waller. With the addition of modern heating and drainage there is no reason why it could not become a viable home.

Walker and McGregor's *The Hebridean Blackhouse* – details in the bibliography – is recommended as a good source for further information.

An overview of a Hebridean blackhouse at Highland Folk Park, Newtonmore, Scotland. Note the thick walls and the roof structure, ready for thatching. All work by staff at the Highland Folk Park.

Beehive Structures

A lintelled or corbelled roof is another option. This produces a round-shaped structure like an old-fashioned bee skep, hence the common name of 'beehive structure'. These buildings are far smaller than a blackhouse because they rely on a lintel or corbelling to enclose the space between the walls. This type of structure is common in Ireland, France and Mediterranean Europe.

In its simplest form a small circular or U-shaped dry stone wall is brought up to 3 or 4ft (1–1.2m).

For the corbelling, additional layers of stone are added, each succeeding course projecting a little more into the interior space. Weight on the tails of the stones, on the outside of the structure, holds them secure.

When the corbelled walls get close enough, lintels, or one flat slab, are used to bridge the space. The top can be finessed with sloping stones, laid so they shed water away to the sides, or a covering of thick sods.

Readers are referred to Renate Löbbecke's excellent website on corbelled domes (*see* bibliography).

A cleit, an example of a beehive structure, one of an estimated thousand on St Kilda, Scottish Hebrides. These are basic versions of a corbelled stone building, of a type found throughout the Celtic fringe and into Europe.

The interior of a St Kildan cleit, showing the arrangement of stones supporting the roof. The outer walls of the cleit are brought up, each succeeding course edging inwards, until they are sufficiently close to accept a lintel. Note the rounding of the corners with obliquely placed stones. The stone walls are laid single, with most of the weight on their outer face. This provides strength and stability.

Chapter Eleven

Modern Walling: Pushing the Boundaries

The mind of the modern waller must be sharper, more attuned to detail and open to innovation. There is still plenty of work in the repair of old walls and the construction of new walls along the traditional patterns, but increasingly the skills of the waller are being called on to create one-off unique pieces.

A modern style of dry stone walling has emerged where higher degrees of accuracy are expected. The stone is often especially selected for the purpose, and carved or cut to suit. The work is more akin to stone-masonry, as in stone and mortar masonry. This new style, with more accurate cutting, shaping and detailing, is reasonably described as 'dry stone masonry'.

The tools for this modern version of the craft are more technical: saws, grinders, laser levels and special chisels are common. The stones are processed to achieve accuracy normally associated with ashlar work, where stone is cut to rectangular shapes with mortar joints as thin as a few millimetres. This tightly jointed work looks good, takes longer to achieve and costs more.

Let it not be understated – this precision, detailed, dry stone work is still governed by the natural laws of friction and gravity. The quality of the final structure is enhanced by greater attention to detail. The practitioners of modern walling are skilled to a higher level but they are using the same fundamental skills developed by those who build the mountain walls of Wales and the boundary dykes in Scotland.

Building Bridges Between Old and New

Dry stone building techniques have never been restricted to agricultural walls; many ancient

A dry stone bridge built in 2016 in Perth, Ontario. Wallers and masons from Canada, Scotland, Ireland and the USA gathered to build this bridge as part of the town's 200th anniversary celebrations. This image shows it nearly complete, apart from work on the deck and the parapets. In 2018, the bridge was recognized as the first National Civil Engineering Demonstration site by The Canadian Society for Civil Engineering. A celebratory plaque tells us: 'This project has demonstrated the art of dry stone masonry, an ancient building technique, and how it can be used in modern day.' This project was conceptualized by John Scott and planned in detail by John Bland.

structures were built of cut stone and no mortar. In modern times, the techniques are being used for the benefit of patrons who appreciate the value of a structure built of natural material, to a high specification and with minimal environmental impact. Dry stone bridges are an excellent opportunity to build something practical, good looking and strong.

A dry stone segmented arch bridge designed by Neil Rippingale and built by a team led by him at the Maker's Mark distillery in Loretto, Kentucky, using 90 tons of Indiana limestone. The total span of the bridge is 20ft (6m). It is 14ft (4.3m) wide, and 10ft (3m) wide inside the parapets.

This interactive public art installation, influenced by a traditional Chinese moon gate, is called 'Moon Bridge'. The structure includes granite recycled from a 100-year-old Vermont bridge. Designed and built by Jared Flynn.

Finessing the Vernacular

This award-winning series of walls, at the approaches to Edinburgh Airport in Scotland, was one of the first artistic dry stone installations in Scotland. These retaining walls were built to imitate and enhance the appearance and effect of dry stone field walls. This work requires skill, concentration and planning to ensure the patterns are maintained. Built by David F. Wilson, designed by David F. Wilson and Keith Horner of Turner Jeffries landscape consultants.

A finely detailed Irish feidín wall, a piece of public art constructed by members and friends of Drystone Canada at one of their stone festivals in 2015.

This wall gives every appearance of being a well-coursed dry stone wall but is actually a veneer onto concrete block. Culloden Battlefield and Visitor Centre, Scotland.

A look at the back side of the Culloden wall confirms the concrete block wall. The property benefits from having an attractive boundary feature without the bulk of a traditional stone wall. Culloden Battlefield and Visitor Centre, Scotland.

Elements from several walling styles are gathered together in a unique piece of land art. Take a few moments to study the build and marvel at its simple complexity. Design and work by Jared Flynn.

Turning the Rules on their Head

The two images here show examples of outstanding craftsmanship from the hands of Sean Donnelly from Ontario, Canada. They are part of a series of six, made from the same 15 tons of stone. Some longer pieces were brought in to add detail and help tie the stonework together. Both structures look unreal.

After getting over initial shock, we realize they are built use the same principles as when they are the right way up, or a complete disc. The creations were supported by a Chalmers Arts Fellowship Award from the Ontario Arts Council. The award aimed to push Sean's abilities as a builder, his concepts of design and his understanding of the elements of the craft.

'Quarter Turn' by Sean Donnelly.

'Upside Down Wall' by Sean Donnelly.

Chapter Twelve

Practical Advice for the Novice

The Building Process

- It is not a jigsaw.
- Lay a stone with its nicest face on the outside, long edge into the wall. Lay it flat and level from side to side and end to end. This makes it easier to build on.
- Lay the face of the stone right up to, but not touching, the string line.
- Once each stone is laid, place hearting under and beside it to secure it and the stones around. Don't leave the hearting until later. Don't move on to another course without first filling in the middle. You can visualize better what to do with each course if the hearting is filled level.
- Break the joints using the principle 'one over two, two over one'. Make sure each stone overlaps the joint between the two stones below it and sits solidly on top of both.
- Don't wander about looking for the perfect stone. Pick up something that looks suitable and consider how it fits into the wall. Lay it. Find another and place it next to the first one. Place a third stone next to the second stone.
- Lay a few stones or a whole course then step back to check if the stones are well fitted together, with no running joints. If a whole course looks reasonable, raise the line and build higher. If it does not look right, rebuild it.
- Use one string line on each side of the wall, set to the average thickness of the stone in the course. One line is easier to follow than two or three on each side. After finishing a course, check the hearting and raise the line. Keep the lines tight and check them often.
- Concentrate on the process, putting quality first. Speed comes with confidence and experience.
- Take your time but don't anguish about every stone. Don't form a committee to discuss how to place a stone.
- Build upwards from the lower courses. Don't place a stone then struggle trying to find something to fit in the gap underneath. Stone goes on top of stone, not under a stone.
- Build tight. Don't chink. Don't fill small places with obliquely placed rubbish. A large stone sitting on a mess of smaller stones will move.
- Stay on your feet, even when working on the foundation. Keep off your knees. Learn to squat. This gives better visibility and mobility, and promotes the body's core strength – that area around the lower back and waist. It is less tiring, makes your back stronger, and reduces the chance of a strain from overreaching.
- Keep your feet clear. Every so often gather the loose stone underfoot and use it for the centre of the wall – it's been picked over enough and is ready for use as hearting. Alternatively, throw these stones away from the wall and allow others to present themselves. Tidy up the site at break times, leaving tools tidily on the wall; you never know who will walk past.

A Promising Start

This short section of retaining wall was built by a complete novice at a stone festival in Ireland. Perseverance and attention to detail produced a reasonable piece of work.

The festival offered a chance to learn the principles of dry stone construction, using good material, with guidance from experienced wallers. Each participant had their own section to work on, at their own pace. There is a physical challenge to dry stone walling, maybe a mental one too, trying to visualize the three-dimensional nature of the work. The novice should trust the process. In the simplest of terms, that means laying each stone properly and being guided by the line.

Short section of retaining wall built by a complete novice.

Tools

- Start off with a basic set of tools and look after them. Keep it simple: a couple of hammers, a pointed chisel, lines, tape measure, a level and a bucket to carry them in is all you really need. Learn how to use those tools properly. Buy better tools as you gain experience.
- Learn how to use a hammer efficiently. A good, heavy brick hammer is as useful, and easier to use, than a chisel.
- Don't be over-enthusiastic with hammers. Shield others from flying chips. The most dangerous thing on a site is an unsupervised seventeen-year-old with a 10lb hammer.
- Don't overwork the stone. Some wallers don't use a hammer very much, especially when repairing a gap. Do not hammer stones once they are on the wall.

Self-Improvement

- Build your first walls in the back of the house, away from the public eye.

- Try to get on a two- or three-day training course. On day two there will be an obvious improvement. On day three you will disown the first day's work. These courses allow like-minded beginners to work together under expert tuition, and also provide an opportunity to gain advice on tools and where to get stone. Details of walling organizations who offer training are given at the end of this book.
- The best way to learn is on old walls. The stones are all at hand; shaping was done years ago. You 'just' need to reassemble them. It can be dispiriting learning how to build a wall from a pile of fresh rock, when you are faced with the twin tasks of learning how to shape the stones and learning how to build a wall from them.
- If you can, start walling with thinner, flatter stone and learn how to lay stone using the accepted mantra of 'one over two; two over one'. Move up to rounded stone then on to broken stone of variable size. Different stones require a different mindset. Some experienced wallers work for years on one type of stone and take a day or two to get used to another type.

- Don't break a good stone, such as a long or a flat one. It will be useful somewhere else, not necessarily on the current wall. Breaking up big stones for hearting is a displacement activity, to distract from the complex task of laying stone.
- Dry stone walling is not a trial of strength, it is a test of concentration and analysis, which has been compared to a choreographed dance. You will probably never match the nimble tread of the feet of Fred Astaire, but aim for economy of movement and efficiency of output.
- The principles of dry stone construction are fixed. Start by learning the basics, considering them as absolute rules. Then learn how to break them and be creative.

Chapter Thirteen

A Final Challenge

We return to the image below for a final challenge. Could you repair this structure? This remarkable old sheep stell includes:

- A combination of single and double build
- Three wall ends, at the end of each 'leg'
- A circular enclosure
- Two wall ends to form the entrance
- Three sections where a straight wall links into the circular wall

- Construction across and up a slope
- Construction on undulating ground

Each of these elements is straightforward by itself, but in combination they need some thought and organization to deal with. The stone is already on site, or easily gathered from the hillside. A crew of competent wallers should be able to go to this site and repair, even replicate, this stell, using a few hand tools, some timber and a string line.

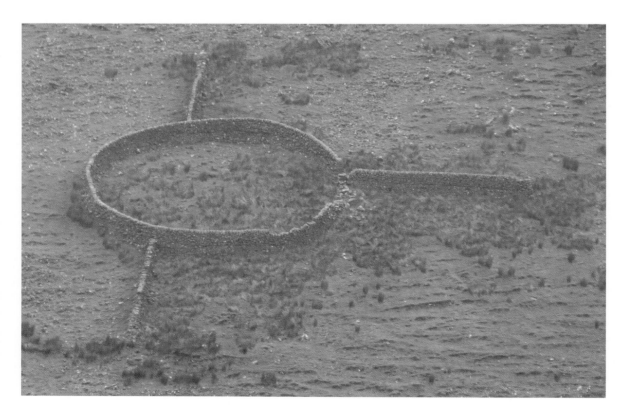

A stell, a storm refuge for sheep. Galtee Mountains, Ireland.

A close-up of part of the stonework in the Irish stell. This is a variation of the Scottish Galloway dyke; it may have been built by Scottish shepherds in the late nineteenth century. Galtee Mountains, Ireland.

A-frame Also known as a batter frame. The profile of a wall, usually built out of timber or reinforcing bar. It looks like a truncated capital letter A. String lines are stretched between two of these frames to indicate the line and batter of the wall

Batter/camber The tapering of the inward slope of a dry stone wall from wide base to narrower top. Typically, a wall tapers 1in (2.5cm) for every 6in (15cm) of a rise – one in six – giving approximately a 10 per cent angle

Bookend A situation in a wall where smaller stones are held securely by a larger one, similar to the way a bookend stops books from toppling

Breaking the joint *See* running joint

Capstone A flat stone laid across the top of a dry stone wall, a type of cope. Typical of New England walls. The term is also used for the top stone of a pillar, usually a flat cap that protects the work below

Cope/copestone The top stones of a wall, typically set vertically or canted to one side. The term 'cope' can describe the whole arrangement of copestones on the top of the wall or one particular stone

Corbelling A method of laying stones to create a roof and enclose a space. Over several courses, the stones project a little more into the space each time, over-hanging it until they meet in the middle or can be bridged with lintels or a flat slab

Course One particular horizontal layer of stones. 'Coursed' is a description of stonework where the size of stones, or combination of stones, in one layer or all the layers are the same. 'Coursing' is a more general description of the way layers of stone are laid – usually with the largest at the bottom, and smaller sizes nearer the top

Coverstone One of the, usually flat, stones that sits along the full length of the wall, on top of the double. Often shortened to 'a cover' when describing one stone or 'the cover' when describing the entire course. 'Coverband' is another term for the entire course – a band of covers

Double dyke/double wall/double-faced A wall type with a foundation, two outer faces ('double-skinned'), usually with throughstones connecting the outer faces and an arrangement of coverstones and copestones on top. Small stones (hearting) in the middle secure the face stones. The body of the wall, that part made up of two outer faces between foundation and cov-erstones, is called 'the double'. The construction and final appearance of the wall depends on what stone is available

Dry A description of stonework built without mortar. A dry stone wall, or drystane dyke in Scottish, is a wall built without mortar. Proper placement of stones, to maximize the effects of friction and gravity, easily compensates for lack of any glue or fixative

Dyker/dry stone dyker/drystane dyker – Scottish term for a dry stone waller

Edge/wedge walling Walls with stones laid upright, on edge, canted or vertical. The stones usually lie with a long edge across the width of the wall

Face stones The stones visible on the side of a wall, those that face out

Falsework/abutments The temporary framework, usually timber, that supports an arch while under construction

Flagstone fence A stone wall made of large, thin, flat stones, set on edge with their length along the length of the fence

Foundation The first course of stone, sitting on the ground. It supports the whole weight of the wall

Free-standing wall A two-sided wall that stands on its own, supporting itself

Headers The long stone at wall ends or openings in the wall; their length lies along the wall

Hearting The small angular stones inside the wall that secure the larger stones. Also known as fill, shims, wedges or packing. A wall properly filled with hearting is said to be 'well-hearted'

Jumper A stone that is taller than others in the course; it 'jumps' up into the level above

Lifts Two sections of the body of the wall. The first lift is between the foundation and the throughstone, and the second lift lies between the throughstone and the top of the double.

Lintel A long stone laid over an opening. Typically found in a lunky

Locked top A style of vertical cope, reputedly invented in southwest Scotland in the 1750s (Rainsford-Hannay, 1976). Flat stones are laid on edge, on top of the double or the coverstones. Thin shims, hammered between the uprights, lock the stones tight

Lunky A low opening in a wall with two vertical sides and a lintel. It allows small animals through but restricts others.

Pinning Small stones, an alternative name for hearting. They support larger stones and fill spaces between the face stones. 'Front pinning' describes the use of small stones on the face of the wall to support larger ones. They are worthless unless placed with care and reach well into the wall

Puddle cap A coping style consisting of small stones piled to a peak, sometimes between spaced-out conventional copestones; a coping option when there is a scarcity of large stones

Racked back/raked back The temporary end of a wall under construction, leaning back at an angle, ready for the next section.

Random Stonework laid with little or no intention to have regularly sized stone set in strict layers. The term describes the way the stones are fitted together. The wall can be just as strong, or stronger, than coursed work

Running joint/rising joint A building fault, usually visible as an unbroken vertical line in the face of a wall. It is caused by not breaking the joint over two or three courses – not following the principle of 'one over two, two over one'. A zipper joint is a situation where the stones overlap, but only just; it looks like a clothing zip

Scarcement A foundation course where the stones extend a few inches beyond the face of the wall. This provides a wider footprint for the wall and adds stability

Sheep dyke The name given to the style of substantial dry stone walls, specifically the Galloway dyke, that came out of southwest Scotland in the 1700s

Shiners/soldiers/sailors Individual stones set vertically in the face of a wall, perhaps as a decorative feature, but more often a second-rate way of closing up a short gap

Single Referring to a whole wall or that part of the wall that is 'single-skinned' or 'single work'. This is only one stone wide. The stones are laid with their length across the width of the wall, largest at the bottom with smaller stones above that, up to a level top line.

Springers The stones on either side of an arch from where the ring stones start or 'spring'

Stepped walling Stonework with a 'jagged' face, looking like a staircase, not flush or keeping to the batter

Stretcher The long stone at a wall end or opening that lies across the width of the wall

Tail That end of a face stone that lies in the middle of the wall

Throughstone/through The long stone that lies across the width of a double wall at regular intervals. It connects the outer edges and adds strength and stability

Traced/traced walling A description of an individual stone, or group of stones, with their longest edge laid along the length of the wall instead of towards the middle of the wall. This is a weak way of building

Wall end/wall head/cheek end (Scottish) The end of a wall, built strong with headers and stretchers

The following is a representative selection, most of which should still be readily available. The reader is recommended to read these as a source for more details on particular aspects of dry stone walling, dry stone structures and the history of walling.

Adcock, S., *Stonework, a Technical Guide to Standards and Identification of Common Faults in Dry Stone Walling* (North Wales Branch of the Dry Stone Walling Association, 2012)

Aitken, N. *Drystone, A Gathering of Terminology and Technique* (Rymour, proposed 2022)

Brooks, A. and Adcock, S., edited by Agate, E., *Dry Stone Walling, a Practical Handbook*, second edition (BTCV, 1999)

Callander, R., *Drystane Dyking in Deeside* (self-published, revised edition 1986)

Copsey, N., *Hot Mixed Lime and Traditional Mortars, a Practical Guide to their Use in Conservation and Repair* (The Crowood Press, 2019)

DSWA, *Walls and the Landscape, a Guide to British Walls* (Dry Stone Walling Association of Great Britain, 2006)

Fields, C.P., *The Forgotten Art of Building a Stone Wall* (Yankee Inc., 1971)

Gardner, K., *The Granite Kiss: Traditions and Techniques of Building New England Stone Walls* (The Countryman Press, 2001)

Garner, L., *Dry Stone Walls* (Shire Publications Ltd, 2005)

Goldsworthy, A., *Wall at Storm King* (Thames & Hudson, 2000)

HES (Historic Environment Scotland), Statement of Significance: Dun Telve (reviewed 2020)

HES (Historic Environment Scotland), Scheduled Monument: Kingswells Consumption Dykes, http://portal.historicenvironment.scot/designation/SM108 (2008)

Hodges, R., *Wall-to-Wall History: the Story of Roystone Grange* (Duckworth, 1991)

Laheen, M., *Drystone Walls of the Aran Islands, Exploring the Cultural Landscape* (The Collins Press, 2010)

Lassure, C., *Building a Drystone Hut: an Instruction Manual*, second edition (Centre d'études et recherches d'architecture vernaculaire (CERAV), 2009)

Lord, T.C., 'One on Two, and Two on One: Preliminary Results from a Survey of Dry Stone Walls on the National Trust Estate at Malham' in White, R. and Wilson, P. eds, *Archaeology and Historic Landscapes in the Yorkshire Dales* (Yorkshire Archaeological Society Occasional Paper No. 2, 2004, pp. 173–186)

McAfee, P., *Irish Stone Walls* (The O'Brien Press Ltd, 2011)

MacWeeney, A. and Conniff, R., *Ireland: Stone Walls and Fabled Landscapes* (Frances Lincoln Limited, 1998)

Mader, G. and Zimmermann, E., *Walls – Elements of Garden and Landscape Architecture* (W.W. Norton & Company Inc., 2011)

Müller, G., *Europe's Field Boundaries* (Neuer Kunstverlag, 2013)

Munday, B., *Those Dry-Stone Walls: Stories from South Australia's Stone Age* (Wakefield Press, 2012)

Murray-Wooley, C. and Raitz, K., *Rock Fences of the Bluegrass* (University Press of Kentucky, 1992)

O'Reilly, M. and Perry, J., *Drystone retaining walls and their modifications – Condition Appraisal and Remedial Treatment* (Construction Industry Research and Information Association (CIRIA), 2009)

Rainsford-Hannay, Col. F., *Dry Stone Walling*, third edition (Stewartry of Kirkcudbright Drystane Dyking Committee, 1976)

Raistrick, A., *The Pennine Walls* (Dalesman Books, 1973)

Robson, M., *Dykes, Ditches and Disputes, a History of Boundary and Field Enclosures in the Borders* (Michael Robson, 2004)

Scully, S., *Walls of Aran* (Thames & Hudson, 2019)

Snow, D., *In the Company of Stone: the Art of the Stone Wall* (Artisan, 2001)

Stell, G.P. and Harman, M., *Buildings of St Kilda* (The Royal Commission on the Ancient and Historical Monuments of Scotland, (RCAHMS), 1988)

Trautwine, J.C. and J.C. Jnr, *The Civil Engineer's Reference-Book,* 21st edition (C.E. Trautwine Company, 1937)

Walker, B. and McGregor, C., *The Hebridean Blackhouse, a Guide to Materials, Construction and Maintenance* (Historic Scotland, Technical Advice Note 5, 1996)

Websites

https://caminsdepedra.conselldemallorca.cat/en/dry-stone-work
For an insight into dry stone walling in Mallorca, connections with European dry stone organizations and opportunities for training

https://canmore.org.uk/site/14279/balnuaran-of-clava-south-west
More details of Clava Cairns

www.cornishhedges.co.uk
For more information of Cornish hedges

www.drystonewalling.wales/wp-content/uploads/2017/01/ClawddConstruction.pdf
For more information on Welsh *clawdd*

www.pierreseche.com (L'architecture en Pierre Seche)
A French website providing comprehensive access to research into dry stone architecture

www.renateloebbecke.de/corbelled-domes
Renate Löbbecke's website Domes offers a full description of corbelled dry stone structures throughout Europe, including the Scottish Hebrides

www.thebrochproject.co.uk
Proposals and plans to recreate a broch

It is worthwhile joining one or more of the following organizations. Check out the websites for membership benefits and access to national and international drystone opportunities.

Training in dry stone walling is accessible throughout Europe, North America and Australia. The following websites include information on dry stone walling and opportunities to participate in training events. Some of the training is on dedicated sites; other training is associated with conservation projects, for example rebuilding old retaining walls. Courses may last a day, two days or longer.

The Dry Stone Walling Association of Great Britain (DSWA)

www.dswa.org.uk

DSWA's website gives contact details for DSWA groups from Central Scotland to Southwest England. DSWA branches also organize walling competitions throughout the country. These are a great opportunity to watch some of the world's best in action.

The Dry Stone Wall Association of Ireland

www.dswai.ie

Training courses, including special ones for agricultural walls, are offered throughout Ireland.

The Dry Stone Walls Association of Australia, Inc.

www.dswaa.org.au

The association increases awareness of historically important walls and offers training on repairs to heritage walls and construction of new walls.

The Stone Trust

https://thestonetrust.org

Based in Vermont, New England, the Stone Trust offers training towards DSWA certification throughout the northeastern USA.

Dry Stone Conservancy (DSC)

www.drystone.org

Primarily based in Kentucky but offering training and certification throughout USA, the DSC also has occasional opportunities for on-the-job training.

Dry Stone Canada

https://drystonecanada.com

Based in eastern Canada, this association offers opportunities to work on public projects and training towards certification from DSC and DSWA levels.

Artisans Batisseurs en Pierres Seches

www.pierreseche.fr

This dry stone wall association is based in southwest France.

The Conservation Volunteers

www.tcv.org.uk

This British organization offers insight and training on many outdoor and environmental topics, including dry stone walling and hedging.

The Stone Foundation

www.stonefoundation.org

In their own words, this organization based in New Mexico, USA, is 'a community of stonemasons and others involved with and/or interested in stone, stonework and stone art.'

A-frames 27–31, 60, 63, 98, 108, 114, 123, 124, 156
agricultural walls 7
ancient walls 7
arches 164–168
    falsework 165–168, 185
    keystone 165–168
    moon gate 168, 174
    small–scale arches 166
    voussoirs or ring stones 164–168

Bailey Island Bridge, Maine 97
batter 7, 9, 12, 27–29, 32, 46–47, 51, 57, 58, 85, 104,
    105, 114, 119, 121–122, 123, 153, 156, 185
bonding patterns 39, 87, 88–97
boulders 10–11, 16, 22, 26, 27, 38, 48, 52, 53, 54, 58,
    71, 69, 85, 88, 89, 92, 93, 95, 98, 99, 112, 124, 127,
    129, 149
breaking/splitting stone (see also trimming stone)
    11, 20, 26–27, 89, 182
brochs 118–119, 188

Caithness flagstone 53, 72, 73, 74, 84, 91, 108,
    117, 133,
capstone 34, 78, 156, 185
curves, circles and arcs 114–117
Clava Cairns 104, 188
clawdd 104, 105, 188
consumption walls 102–104
copestones 20, 21, 26, 28–29, 52, 69–79, 108, 128, 185
    adding height 80–82
    agricultural walls 70
    bad coping 62, 137
    exaggerated copes, Galloway dyke and feidín
        wall 98–101
    height of 70
    in combination with the coverband 67–68, 86
    locked top 70–71
    mortared copestones 136, 137
    on double walls 10, 38
    on slopes 78, 126
    puddle cap 69
    topping off retaining walls 156
    vertical cope 83, 130, 132
    while repairing a gap 142–150
Cornish hedges 104, 188
coursed walling 66, 83–84, 86, 153, 175, 185
    badly coursed work 62, 87
corners
    curved corners 121–122, 169, 171
    square corners 119–121, 169

coverstones/coverband/covers 26, 38, 51, 66–69, 80,
    85, 86
    calculating requirement 21
    on curves 114
    while repairing a gap 144–148
cross-section of typical wall 38, 46, 47, 51, 146

dips and hollows, building across 123
double wall/dyke 10, 38, 51, 88, 89, 92, 93, 96, 123,
    126, 185
dry stone masonry 172

face stones 10, 17, 22, 30, 39, 46, 48, 49, 51, 54, 55, 57,
    59, 62, 63, 66, 67, 71, 79, 115, 121, 124, 144, 145,
    146, 148, 152, 185
feidín wall 11, 69, 98, 100–101, 175
first lift 51, 59–63, 66, 147, 186
foundation
    digging the founds 52
    drainage and obstacles 57–59
    failed foundations 58
    flexible rigidity 52–53
    floating stone 57
    frost heave 57
    gravel as a base 157
    ground pressure 54
    laying stone 54
    on slopes 59
    retaining wall foundations 156
    scarcements 54
freestanding walls 8, 50, 132
frost and frost heave 19, 57, 61, 128, 136,
    and drainage for retaining walls 157,

gabion baskets 104–107
Galloway dyke 69, 98–101, 184, 186
gapping, repairing a collapse
    rebuild sequence 142–148
    use of lines and frames 146
gravel, reasons not to use 48, 58, 154,

health and safety 23–24
hearting 9, 10, 22, 30, 38, 39, 43, 44, 47–49, 51, 54,
    58, 59, 61, 67, 93, 100, 114, 121, 135, 144, 146, 147,
    148, 153, 154, 180, 185
herringbone pattern 132

Irish limestone 14, 94–96, 162,

Kingswells Consumption Dyke 104

laying stone
    badly laid stone 58, 62
    basic guidance 39
    floaters and riders 39–40
    in first lift 59–63
    in second lift 66–67
    lay up to line 32
    laying the foundation 54
    on edge 40–45, 128–134
    shiners, soldiers and sailors 45
    single and double walls 38
lines and strings *see* string lines

modern walling 172–179
mortars
    justification for the term 'dry' 7–9, 38, 185
    mortared cope 75, 76, 136, 137, 156
    use in dry stone walls 83, 135–136

novice, practical advice for 180–182

openings
    bee bole 164
    lintelled openings 156, 159, 160 –164, 170, 171, 186
    squeeze stile 163
    the lunky 100, 156, 159, 163, 164, 169, 186

pinning and front pinning 46, 49, 63, 121, 186

random coursing 83, 85–87, 186
retaining walls 148, 157
    foundations 156
    free draining nature 157
    frost heave 157
    recommended dimensions 152
    theory of 152
    topping off 156
    types 153–156
    use of fabric and/or gravel 158
    use of lines and frames 154, 156
rock types and origins
    igneous 13–14, 16
    metamorphic 13, 16, 27
    sedimentary 14–16, 27, 60
roofing stone structures
    beehive structures 170
    Hebridean blackhouse 169

second lift 51, 66–68, 147, 186
single walling 10, 11, 16, 38, 39, 88, 94, 95, 98, 112, 123, 147, 186
slabs of rock and stone pillars 132–134
slopes and inclines
    building on dips hollows and slopes 83, 123–128
    coping on a slope 78
    foundation on slopes 54, 59
sourcing stone
    cost 18, 20, 97, 152
    old structures 17
    pallets 20
    quarries 20
    selecting stone 18
    suitable stones 20–22
stone-faced earth banks 104, 105
string lines
    avoid overuse in complex structures 114
    for curved corners 122
    for foundation 54, 56, 58
    for Galloway dyke and feidín wall 98
    for half-round pillar or plinth 34
    for pyramids 34
    for repairing gaps 145–146
    for round pillars and cones 34
    for square corners 119, 121
    for square pillars 32–34
    for steep slopes 124
    for wall ends 112
    general use 24, 27, 28, 29, 31, 59, 60, 63, 65, 66, 69, 83, 84–86, 180, 185
    in random walling 85

throughstones/throughs 63–66, 186
tools 24–25, 26–27, 172, 181
tower building 49
traced stone 39–40, 44–45, 58, 67, 113, 186
trees, dealing with trees and tree roots 52, 59, 136–141, 146, 146, 167
trimming stone (see also breaking stone) 26, 27, 45–47, 60, 68
Triumph of the Wall (2013 documentary film) 34
turf and stone dyke 8, 9

urbanite 16–17